AMIGURUMI
CROCHET

AMIGURUMI
CROCHET

Super-cute patterns for animals, sea creatures, sweet treats and more

LAURA STRUTT

CICO BOOKS

LONDON NEW YORK

For Ethan Wolf & Elkie Raven – fiercely & forever.

Published in 2024 by CICO Books
an imprint of Ryland Peters & Small Ltd
20–21 Jockey's Fields, London WC1R 4BW

www.rylandpeters.com

10 9 8 7 6 5 4 3 2 1

A CIP catalogue record for this book
is available from the British Library.

ISBN: 978 1 80065 342 9

Printed in China

Editor: Marie Clayton
Pattern checker: Jemima Bicknell
Designer: Alison Fenton
Photographer: Geoff Dann
Materials and tools photography
on pages 8–10: James Gardiner
Stylist: Nel Haynes
Illustrator: Stephen Dew

In-house editor: Jenny Dye
Art director: Sally Powell
Creative director: Leslie Harrington
Head of production: Patricia Harrington
Publishing manager: Carmel Edmonds

CONTENTS

INTRODUCTION

Amigurumi (pronounced: ami-gu-ru-mi) is Japanese and translates as 'crocheted stuffed toy'. This technique uses only a couple of stitches – predominantly double crochet (US single crochet) – and is worked in the round in a continuous spiral. The shapes of the characters are built by increasing or decreasing stitches as the rounds are worked. Almost like yarn caricatures, these little projects soon take on huge personalities with their exaggerated elements and the addition of shiny little black eyes and sweet stitched features.

In this collection I have included a host of fun makes from foods and day-to-day items to under-the-sea and woodland characters. Plus, there is a chapter of supersize designs to show you how to imagine these small characters into a larger-than-life format. The projects feature a range of staple shapes found in amigurumi, from spheres and cones to cylinders, spirals and more! Not only can you use the patterns to recreate these fun characters, but you can also use the different elements to inspire you to design your very own amigurumi creatures.

I hope that the selection of amigurumi characters in this book give you just as much joy to crochet as they gave me to create them. Happy crocheting!

My very first introduction to amigurumi was when I was working as Deputy Editor on a popular knitting magazine. Having only previously crocheted granny squares, I was delighted to discover that you could create little characters that are jam-packed with personality using one simple crochet stitch and some toy stuffing. Not only could you crochet dolls and teddies, but I soon realised that you could use this crochet style to create characters of anything that takes your fancy – needless to say, I was hooked!

Before you begin

If you are new to crochet or amigurumi, or if you come across a technique you don't understand, please check out the Abbreviations list on page 126, the tips on working amigurumi on page 11, and the Techniques section on pages 118–125.

For information about the amount of yarn you will need, see Cotton DK (Light Worsted) yarn and Chunky (bulky) chenille yarn opposite.

Each of the projects has a skill rating:
● ○ ○ Quick Make: these projects are single or simple shapes that can be worked quickly and easily.
● ● ○ Weekend Project: these patterns feature a few different elements that need to be combined to create the finished character.
● ● ● Challenge Yourself: these characters require you to dedicate more time to work their more involved techniques or create their multiple elements.

MATERIALS

YARNS AND THREADS
Most of the projects in this book are worked with Cotton DK (light worsted) yarn, although the larger figures are made in chenille yarn. Details are added with perlé cotton.

Cotton DK (light worsted) yarn
DK or double knitting (light worsted) is a great weight of yarn for amigurumi because it is thin enough to allow you to create lots of details, yet not so fine that it is tricky for beginners to handle. It is also one of the most popular yarn weights so it is available in a huge range of colours, and you may already have some in your yarn stash.

These projects have been worked in a 100% cotton DK, which is a soft and strong yarn. Because a 100% cotton yarn has less stretch than a blended or acrylic yarn, it makes a very sturdy and consistent fabric when crocheting amigurumi. Many beginners find that maintaining tension (gauge) is easier with a cotton yarn over a blended yarn. You can, of course, also work with a mixture of cotton and acrylic yarns in your projects; however, you will need to be mindful that these yarns will have different finishes and you may need to swatch each of them first to ensure that they create the same finished tension (see page 11).

You don't have to work with a single brand of yarn for the entire project you're making. This is a huge plus because you can shop around (or in your stash!) and pick the right colour and finish for each element. It is wise to swatch each of the yarns from different brands though, to be sure that you achieve the same finish or to identify whether you need to vary the hook size. Due to the scale of the projects In Chapters 1 to 4, they don't require vast amounts of yarn. Some projects will require multiple colours but they won't use more than a 50g (1¾oz) ball, or 25g (1oz) amount in many cases, for each colour. This is great because you can use yarns in your stash or select from a wide range of brands that offer cotton DK in both 50g (1¾oz) balls and 20–25g (¾–1oz) balls.

Chunky (bulky) chenille yarn
This type of yarn is both bulky and ultra-soft. It is made with a twisted construction, where the synthetic fibres of the yarn are twisted around an inner core. These fluffy fibres give the yarn a plush 'pile' around its entire length.

With its fuzzy finish, this yarn is an ideal choice for the plush supersized amigurumi projects in Chapter 5. However, its fluffy nature means that it can shed when the yarn is cut. Tying a knot at the cut ends secures it and prevents the yarn from fraying. Chenille yarn can be tricky to unpick if you need to take out some stitches; if you need to undo stitches, working slowly and undoing one stitch at a time is the best way to avoid damaging the yarn pile. Also, because it is such a dense yarn, it can sometimes be tricky to see the stitches, especially if you are working with a dark shade or black yarn. Be sure to work in good light to prevent eye strain or making mistakes with the stitches.

Chenille yarn is chunky and you will need to size up to a larger hook, so it may be worth making a few test swatches to get the right hook size. The chenille yarn I used came in 100g (3½oz) balls, but you will only need smaller amounts for some colours.

Perlé cotton

Perlé cotton, also called mercerized cotton, is usually found in the embroidery section of craft shops and online retailers and is available in a wide range of colours. 'Mercerized' is the term for the chemical process during manufacture that gives the thread a lustrous sheen. While you can use other embroidery threads (floss) or yarns for adding the face details to amigurumi projects, my preference is to work with perlé cotton. The lush sheen gives a great finish to the fine details of the project, and the firm twist construction means that strands don't tend to get fluffy or kink on the surface of the work. Unlike embroidery threads, where you can extract the number of required strands to create the desired thickness of your stitches, perlé cotton is a non-divisible thread. This means you can't break it down into separate strands, but it is available in a range of weights or thicknesses: No.3, No.5, No.8 and No. 2. Number 3 is the heaviest/thickest weight and 12 is the lightest/finest thread. These projects use a No.8 weight perlé cotton.

OTHER MATERIALS

Safety eyes

Safety eyes are two-part plastic eyes that are pushed through from the front, or right side, of the character, then the second element is secured firmly onto the inside, or wrong side (see page 124). Always ensure that safety eyes are fastened securely. Buttons, beads or sequins can also be used to create the eyes, but if you are making these characters for children or small babies, omit the safety eyes (or buttons, beads or sequins) and just use threads or yarns to stitch the accents.

Toy stuffing

While you can use any soft padding material to fill your characters, purpose-made toy stuffing is the best option. Work by adding in small pieces at a time, little and often - this will result in a firm full piece without any unsightly lumps or bumps.

Plastic pellets/beads

Some items can benefit from added weight - often at the bottom of the piece - to help them stand. Plastic pellets or beads are commonly used in doll-making and are a great option; they are available from craft and toy-making shops. To prevent the small beads from eventually working through the fabric of the crochet, fill a small fabric pouch (tights are ideal for this!) and knot it firmly before adding to the character at the base, then continue filling with toy stuffing.

Alternatives for plastic beads/pellets

While plastic beads are a great option to give an item stability, you may not wish to include additional plastic in your projects. You might like to try working with glass beads. These are available from craft shops and can be used in much the same way as plastic beads. Securing them in a small pouch will prevent any from leaking out of the piece. Glass beads are heavier than plastic beads so you may only need a small amount to achieve the desired weight.

A store cupboard ingredient that has often been used to stuff toys is dried lentils or beans. Again, securing these in a fabric pouch prevents any of the lentils escaping from the finished amigurumi. It is important to ensure that any dried food items used as stuffing are kept dry, as any exposure to damp could cause mould.

Mylar®

These polyester film sheets are commonly used in craft and stencilling projects and can be beneficial in amigurumi when a completely flat base is required. Mylar® sheets can be cut with a pair of sharp scissors, but make sure there are no sharp corners that could be felt through the crochet. Place a small piece in the base of your amigurumi project before filling it with plastic pellets/beads or stuffing; this gives a smooth flat base to the design.

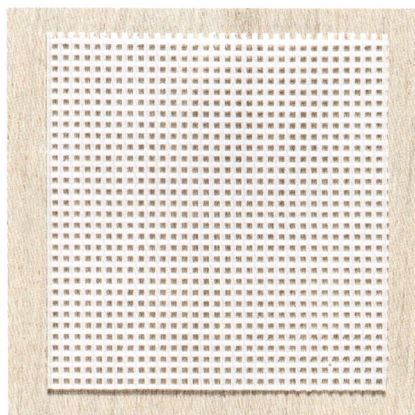

Plastic canvas

Much like Mylar®, plastic canvas is a great option for giving additional structure to an amigurumi project. Plastic canvas is often found in the needlework section of craft shops and is a sheet of plastic with a grid of holes that can be cut to the desired size with sharp scissors. It is much sturdier than Mylar® but it's very lightweight because of the holes. The grid can also be stitched into place, ensuring that supporting pieces don't slip during the construction. Again, make sure there are no sharp corners when cutting the piece.

Alternative ideas for adding structure

While both Mylar® and plastic canvas are great options to create the desired shape or form of an amigurumi piece, you may have alternative items around the house that you could use. Thin plastic from yoghurt pots, food tubs and plastic packaging are all great options. Ensure they are clean and cut carefully to size, and check that any printed elements on the plastic are positioned inwards so they don't show through the crochet fabric. As with Mylar® and plastic canvas, be sure to round off any corners so that a sharp point can't be felt through the work. Stiff cardboard can also be used as a plastic-free alternative. However, this will not be water-resistant, whereas plastic inside a finished piece means that it can be hand washed.

Wire

Both floristry wire and craft wire (15 gauge/1.5mm) are useful for giving amigurumi pieces lasting sculpted shapes. The wires are either inserted into the finished piece or formed into shape and added into the character during the construction process. The use of wires is entirely optional and must be omitted from any item made for children or babies.

TOOLS

These are the basic tools you will need for all the projects in this book.

Crochet hooks

Crochet hooks come in a range of different styles and materials, such as metal (steel or aluminium) plastic, bamboo or wood. The most important thing is to get the right size hook for the project – the aim is to create a fabric that is firm and free from holes and gaps. If you are seeing gaps in your crochet that are large enough that the toy stuffing would show through, this is a sign that you need to go down a size of crochet hook – for example from a 3.25mm (US size D/3) hook to a 3mm (US size C/2–D) hook. However, if you are struggling to get the hook through the stitches and need to use force to draw the yarn through (sometimes you can hear the yarn squeaking against the hook!), this is an indication that you need to try a larger hook – for example instead of a 3.25mm (US size D/3) hook you might like to try a 3.5mm (US size E/4) hook.

Once you have found the hook size to create the tension (gauge) that you desire, be sure to hold the yarn in the same way throughout the project because this will help to maintain an even tension. This may mean that you need a selection of hooks, including both a size up and down from the one suggested in the pattern, to achieve the right tension for you.

When it comes to the style of crochet hooks for amigurumi, as with any form of crochet, this is usually down to personal preference. Metal hooks are often praised for having a more defined point on the head, making it easier to work stitches; however, some people find that they are cold and hard on the hands after repeated use. Plastic hooks, while arguably less durable than metal, have the benefit of being lightweight and are available in a range of colours. Those who suffer from hand pain tend to opt for ergonomic crochet hooks. These are either a plastic-rubber hybrid or a metal-rubber hybrid, which give additional padding and grip for the user.

Many crochet enthusiasts prefer to work with hooks made from natural materials – wood or bamboo – as these are lightweight and warm to the touch, which makes them easy on the hands. However, they can become worn from (very) heavy use and any slight imperfection can snag on the yarn and prevent the smooth flow of making the stitches.

Stitch markers

Locking or ring markers are used to identify the start of the round, to help you keep track of the pattern. These projects have been worked in a continuous spiral (rather than joined rounds) unless specified in the pattern.

Yarn needle

These come in various sizes, but all have large eyes for easy threading of yarn, and a blunt end which will not split the stitches when you are sewing up your work.

Sharp scissors

You will need these for cutting yarn after finishing a piece and when sewing up. It is tempting to break yarn with your hands, but this can pull the stitches out of shape.

Pins

Long rustproof, glass-headed or T-headed quilter's pins can be used to pin crocheted pieces together for sewing up. Bright-coloured tops make it easy to spot the pins against the crocheted fabric so you don't leave any behind!

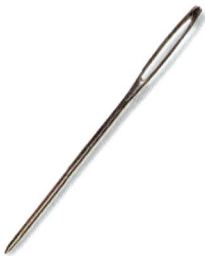

WORKING AMIGURUMI

Here are a few hints and tips that will help you to achieve the best results with your amigurumi projects.

Tension (gauge)

While the specific tension isn't essential for these projects, it is important that the fabric created is firm and helps to hold the toy stuffing in place (see Crochet hooks, opposite).

When it comes to getting the correct tension for amigurumi, the main thing to consider is the finish of the fabric, which needs to be fairly stiff and sturdy. This is what allows It to hold its shape. The gaps in the fabric need to be small too, as this prevents the stuffing from being visible or escaping through the holes. You can work a swatch to see how the chosen hook and yarn affect the finished crocheted fabric. Usually the tension swatch you make needs to be slightly larger than the area given in the tension information at the start of the pattern. For example, for garments a 10cm (4in) measured area is given in the pattern, so the swatch you make would need to be larger than this – a minimum of 12-13cm (4½-5in) square – to check the measurements. For amigurumi you may find that working a small swatch such as 20 stitches by 20 rows in double crochet (US single crochet) will be enough to show what the finished fabric will look like.

If you go on to create your own designs, you may like to swatch up a small sphere as this is a great way to check for the tension of the finished fabric in a 3D shape. It will also help you to design items such as heads, bodies, and different elements of the limbs.

Colour changes

When working with repeated colour changes in the round for amigurumi, you may prefer to carry the yarn inside the work, rather than cut the yarn at each change. To do this, complete the last stitch in the first colour using the new yarn (so the final yarn round hook and pull through of the stitch is worked in the new colour) and carry the previous yarn as the next stitches are worked. You can create 'floats' on the inside of the work by catching the unused yarn against the inside with the working yarn. This has the benefit of holding it out of the way so it is ready for the next colour change. Be sure not to draw the unused yarn too tight because this will pull in the work and affect the finished shape.

Joining elements

While a number of the amigurumi projects in this book are worked as a single element, there are a few that will require seaming together. Using long pins to hold the elements in place before stitching will help you to get the correct position – this is particularly useful if you are adding pieces that need to be symmetrical, for example ears and limbs. Once pinned you can use the yarn tail threaded onto the yarn needle to secure them into place (see page 124). Just before completing the seam, it is a good idea to check the amount of stuffing and take the opportunity to add in a few more pieces if necessary. Areas at joins tend to need firmer stuffing than other sections – this is particularly true of the seam between head and body pieces and adding

extra stuffing here will prevent the head from becoming floppy.

Working with long sections

When projects are small, long sections, such as the Mermaid's hair, can be tricky to work with. See the tip on page 50 for how to make this easier.

Adding features

The faces for the characters in this book are created by using safety eyes (see page 8) and embroidery in perlé cotton or chenille yarn. To add the mouths and cheek details, hand-sew them on using straight stitches (see page 125).

If you opt to omit safety eyes, you can work with threads or yarn to sew the eyes in place. This is a chance to give your amigurumi character your chosen style and personality. For each eye, you can work a single straight stitch, or make a small curved stitch by working a slightly longer straight and catching the centre of the length with a smaller stitch to draw it down into a curve. You may also opt to make the eyes small 'V' shapes, similar to the mouth.

CHAPTER 1

FOODIE FUN

CUPCAKE

Nothing says celebration quite like a cupcake. This pink-topped, caramel-coloured sweet treat is finished with white icing and multicoloured sprinkles.

SKILL RATING ● ● ●

YARN AND MATERIALS

Cotton DK yarn (100% cotton)
  Beige
  Light Pink
  White

Pair of 5–6mm (⅜–¼in) safety eyes

Perlé Cotton No.8 in Black and White

Small scraps/offcuts of other yarns for sprinkles

Mylar® or piece of fairly stiff plastic (optional)

Plastic pellets/beads (optional)

Toy stuffing

HOOK AND EQUIPMENT

3.25mm (US size D/3) crochet hook

Locking or ring stitch marker

Yarn needle

Pins

FINISHED MEASUREMENTS

7.5 x 7.5cm (3 x 3in)

ABBREVIATIONS

See page 126

CUPCAKE BASE

(worked from base upwards)
Using Beige, make a magic ring.
Round 1: 6dc into ring. (*6 sts*)
PM at start of round.
Round 2: [Inv inc in next st] 6 times. (*12 sts*)
Round 3: [1dc in next st, inv inc in next st] 6 times. (*18 sts*)
Round 4: [1dc in next 2 sts, inv inc in next st] 6 times. (*24 sts*)
Round 5: [1dc in next 3 sts, inv inc in next st] 6 times. (*30 sts*)
Round 6: [1dc in next 4 sts, inv inc in next st] 6 times. (*36 sts*)
Round 7: [1dc in next 5 sts, inv inc in next st] 6 times. (*42 sts*)
Round 8: 1dcBLO in each st.
Rounds 9 and 10: 1dc in each st.
Round 11: [1dc in next 6 sts, inv inc in next st] 6 times. (*48 sts*)
Rounds 12–16: 1dc in each st.
Fasten off.

CUPCAKE TOP

Using Light Pink, make a magic ring.
Round 1: 6dc into ring. (*6 sts*)
PM at start of round.
Round 2: [Inv inc in next st] 6 times. (*12 sts*)
Round 3: [1dc in next st, inv inc in next st] 6 times. (*18 sts*)
Round 4: [1dc in next 2 sts, inv inc in next st] 6 times. (*24 sts*)
Round 5: [1dc in next 3 sts, inv inc in next st] 6 times. (*30 sts*)
Round 6: [1dc in next 4 sts, inv inc in next st] 6 times. (*36 sts*)
Round 7: [1dc in next 5 sts, inv inc in next st] 6 times. (*42 sts*)
Round 8: [1dc in next 6 sts, inv inc in next st] 6 times. (*48 sts*)
Rounds 9–14: 1dc in each st.
Round 15: [4trFLO in next st, skip next st, sl st in next st] 16 times.
Fasten off, leaving a long tail for sewing.

ICING

Using White, make a magic ring.

Round 1: 6dc into ring. (*6 sts*)
PM at start of round.

Round 2: [Inv inc in next st] 6 times. (*12 sts*)

Round 3: [1dc in next st, inv inc in next st] 6 times. (*18 sts*)

Round 4: [1dc in next 2 sts, inv inc in next st] 6 times. (*24 sts*)

Round 5: [1dc in next 3 sts, inv inc in next st] 6 times. (*30 sts*)

Round 6: 4tr in next st, skip next st, sl st in next 3 sts, (2tr, 2dtr, 2tr) in next st, skip next st, sl st in next 3 sts, 4tr in next st, skip next st, sl st in next 4 sts, (2tr, 2dtr, 2tr) in next st, skip next st, sl st in next 3 sts, 4tr in next st, skip next st, sl st in next 3 sts, (2tr, 2dtr, 2tr) in next st, skip next st, sl st in last 2 sts.
Fasten off, leaving a long tail for sewing.

MAKING UP AND FINISHING

Position safety eyes at centre front of base and fasten securely (see page 124).

Sew face details using Perlé cotton and yarn needle, using Black for V-shaped mouth and White for cheeks (see page 125). Fasten off and secure all thread ends.

Place icing centrally on top of pink cupcake top, pin in place. Using small lengths of coloured yarn, work a selection of straight stitches through icing and cupcake top to create sprinkles. Thread tail from icing into a yarn needle and work around outer edge to sew in place on cupcake top (see page 124). Fasten off yarn securely and remove pins.

(Optional: Cut a circular piece, approx. 5cm/2in diameter, of Mylar® or fairly stiff plastic and place into base of cupcake. Fill a small fabric bag, or section of tights knotted, with plastic pellets/beads and insert into base to add weight.)

Fill base with toy stuffing, working with small pieces at a time.

Place cupcake upper onto base and pin in place. Thread tail into a yarn needle and join by seaming through unworked back loops of cupcake top and cupcake base. Leave small gap to fill. Add stuffing in small pieces until firm, then complete seam.

Fasten off and bury tail through body of cupcake.

ICE CREAM

With two scoops and whipped cream this ice cream is the perfect indulgence. The cone is worked in a golden yellow with mint and purple for the scoops, topped with a ruffle of white.

SKILL RATING ● ● ○

YARN AND MATERIALS
Cotton DK yarn (100% cotton)
  Gold/Yellow
  Mint
  Purple
  White
Pair of 5-6mm (⅜-¼in) safety eyes
Perlé Cotton No.8 in Black and Pink
Toy stuffing
Mylar® or piece of fairly stiff plastic (optional)
Plastic pellets/beads (optional)

HOOK AND EQUIPMENT
3.25mm (US size D/3) crochet hook
Locking or ring stitch marker
Yarn needle
Pins

FINISHED MEASUREMENTS
6.5 x 15cm (2½ x 6in)

ABBREVIATIONS
See page 126

ICE CREAM CONE
(worked from base upwards)
Using Gold/Yellow, make a magic ring.
Round 1: 6dc into ring. (*6 sts*) PM at start of round.
Round 2: [Inv inc in next st] 6 times. (*12 sts*)
Round 3: [1dc in next st, inv inc in next st] 6 times. (*18 sts*)
Round 4: [1dc in next 2 sts, inv inc in next st] 6 times. (*24 sts*)
Round 5: [1dc in next 3 sts, inv inc in next st] 6 times. (*30 sts*)
Round 6: 1dcBLO in each st.
Rounds 7-14: 1dc in each st.
Round 15: [1dc in next 9 sts, inv inc in next st] 3 times. (*33 sts*)
Rounds 16-19: 1dc in each st.
Round 20: [1dc in next 9 sts, inv dec] 3 times. (*30 sts*)
Fasten off, leaving a long tail for sewing.

LARGE SCOOP

Using Mint, make a magic ring.

Round 1: 10dc into ring. (*10 sts*)
PM at start of round.

Round 2: [Inv inc in next st]
10 times. (*20 sts*)

Round 3: 1dc in each st.

Round 4: [1dc in next st, inv inc
in next st] 10 times. (*30 sts*)

Round 5: [1dc in next 2 sts, inv
inc in next st] 10 times. (*40 sts*)

Rounds 6–12: 1dc in each st.

Round 13: [1dc in next 2 sts, inv dec]
10 times. (*30 sts*)

Round 14: 1dc in each st.

Round 15: 4dcFLO in each st.
(*120 sts*)

Position safety eyes at centre
front of scoop and fasten securely
(see page 124).

Sew face details using Perlé cotton
and yarn needle, using Black for
V-shaped mouth and Pink for
cheeks (see page 125). Fasten off
and secure all thread ends.

SMALL SCOOP

Using Purple, make a magic ring.

Round 1: 10dc into ring. (*10 sts*)
PM at start of round.

Round 2: [Inv inc in next st]
10 times. (*20 sts*)

Round 3: 1dc in each st.

Round 4: [1dc in next st, inv inc
in next st] 10 times. (*30 sts*)

Rounds 5–10: 1dc in each st.

Round 11: [1dc in next st, inv dec]
10 times. (*20 sts*)

Round 12: 1dc in each st.

Round 13: 4dcFLO in each st.
(*80 sts*)

Fasten off, leaving a long tail
for sewing.

WHIPPED CREAM

Using White, make a magic ring.

Round 1: 6dc into ring. (*6 sts*)
PM at start of round.

Round 2: [Inv inc in next st] 6 times.
(*12 sts*)

Round 3: [1dc in next st, inv inc
in next st] 6 times. (*18 sts*)

Fasten off, leaving a long tail
for sewing.

MAKING UP AND FINISHING

Place whipped cream on top of
small scoop and pin in place.
Thread tail into a yarn needle
and sew to secure (see page 124),
then remove pins.

Fill small scoop with toy stuffing,
working with small pieces at a
time. Position small scoop on top
of large scoop and pin in place.
Thread tail into a yarn needle and
sew to secure, then remove pins.
(Optional: Cut a circular piece,
approx. 3.5cm/1½in in diameter,
of Mylar® or fairly stiff plastic
and place into base of cone. Fill
a small fabric bag, or piece of tights
knotted, with some plastic pellets/
beads and insert into base to
add weight.)

Fill base with toy stuffing, working
with small pieces at a time.
Place large scoop onto cone and
pin in place. Thread tail into a yarn
needle and join by sewing through
unworked back loops of large scoop
and cone. Leave a small gap to fill.
Add stuffing in small pieces until
firm, then complete seam and
remove pins.

Fasten off and bury tail through
body of ice cream.

SUSHI

This savoury trio features sushi favourites: Maki, Tamago Nigiri and Shrimp Nigiri. They are created with black and white yarns with accents of rust, coral, yellow and green.

SKILL RATING ● ● ●

YARN AND MATERIALS

Cotton DK yarn (100% cotton)
  Rust
  White
  Black
  Yellow
  Coral

Small scraps/offcuts of Bright Green and Light Pink for accents

Three pairs of of 5–6mm (⅜–¼in) safety eyes

Perlé Cotton No.8 in Black and Pink

Toy stuffing

Mylar® or piece of fairly stiff plastic (optional)

HOOK AND EQUIPMENT

3.25mm (US size D/3) crochet hook

Locking or ring stitch marker

Yarn needle

FINISHED MEASUREMENTS

Maki: 5 x 4cm (2 x 1½in)

Tamago Nigiri: 7.5 x 5cm (3 x 2in)

Shrimp Nigiri: 7.5 x 5cm (3 x 2in)

ABBREVIATIONS

See page 126

MAKI (PICTURED ABOVE LEFT)

Using Rust, make a magic ring.

Round 1: 6dc into ring. (*6 sts*)
PM at start of round.

Round 2: [Inv inc in next st] 6 times. (*12 sts*)

Round 3: [1dc in next st, inv inc in next st] 6 times. (*18 sts*)

Round 4: Inv colour change to White, [1dc in next 2 sts, inv inc in next st] 6 times. (*24 sts*)

Round 5: [1dc in next 3 sts, inv inc in next st] 6 times. (*30 sts*)

Round 6: Inv colour change to Black, [1dc in next 4 sts, inv inc in next st] 6 times. (*36 sts*)

Round 7: 1dcBLO in each st.
Position safety eyes at centre of circle and fasten securely (see page 124).
Sew face details using Perlé cotton and yarn needle, using Black for V-shaped mouth and Pink for cheeks (see page 125). Fasten off and secure all thread ends.

Rounds 8–14: 1dc in each st.

Round 15: 1dcBLO in each st.

Round 16: [1dc in next 4 sts, inv dec] 6 times. (*30 sts*)

Round 17: [1dc in next 3 sts, inv dec] 6 times. (*24 sts*)
Fill with small pieces of toy stuffing. (Optional: Cut circular piece of Mylar® or fairly stiff plastic and place into front of roll to fit neatly around backs of safety eyes.)

Round 18: [1dc in next 2 sts, inv dec] 6 times. (*18 sts*)

Round 19: [1dc in next st, inv dec] 6 times. (*12 sts*)

Round 20: [Inv dec] 6 times. (*6 sts*)
Fasten off.
Cut yarn, thread tail into a yarn needle and close opening by weaving through front loops only. Fasten off and bury tail through body of maki.

MAKING UP AND FINISHING

Use a small amount of Bright Green to add wasabi accent.

TAMAGO NIGIRI (PICTURED BELOW RIGHT)

NIGIRI RICE

(make 1)

Using White, ch10.

Round 1: Beg in 2nd ch from hook, 1dc in next 8 ch, 3dc in last ch, cont down opp side of chain with 1dc in next 7 sts, 2dc in last ch. (20 sts) PM at start of round.

Round 2: Inv inc in next st, 1dc in next 7 sts, inv inc in each of next 3 sts, 1dc in next 7 sts, inv inc in each of next 2 sts. (26 sts)

Round 3: 1dc in next st, inv inc in next st, 1dc in next 7 sts, [1dc in next st, inv inc in next st] 3 times, 1dc in next 7 sts, [1dc in next st, inv inc in next st] twice. (32 sts)

Round 4: 1dc in next 2 sts, inv inc in next st, 1dc in next 7 sts, [1dc in next 2 sts, inv inc in next st] 3 times, 1dc in next 7 sts, [1dc in next 2 sts, inv inc in next st] twice. (38 sts)

Round 5: 1dc in next 3 sts, inv inc in next st, 1dc in next 7 sts, [1dc in next 3 sts, inv inc in next st] 3 times, 1dc in next 7 sts, [1dc in next 3 sts, inv inc in next st] twice. (44 sts)

Round 6: 1dcBLO in each st.

Rounds 7–10: 1dc in each st.

Position safety eyes in centre of end and fasten securely.

Sew face details using Perlé cotton and yarn needle, using Black for V-shaped mouth and Pink for cheeks. Fasten off and secure all thread ends.

Round 11: 1dcBLO in each st.

Round 12: 1dc in next 3 sts, inv dec, 1dc in next 7 sts, [1dc in next 3 sts, inv dec] 3 times, 1dc in next 7 sts, [1dc in next 3 sts, inv dec] twice. (38 sts)

Round 13: 1dc in next 2 sts, inv dec, 1dc in next 7 sts, [1dc in next 2 sts, inv dec] 3 times, 1dc in next 7 sts, [1dc in next 2 sts, inv dec] twice. (32 sts)

Beg filling with small pieces of toy stuffing, cont adding as dec rounds are worked.

Round 14: 1dc in next st, inv dec, 1dc in next 7 sts, [1dc in next st, inv dec] 3 times, 1dc in next 7 sts, [1dc in next st, inv dec] twice. (26 sts)

Round 15: Inv dec, 1dc in next 7 sts, [inv dec] 3 times, 1dc in next 7 sts, [inv dec] twice. (20 sts)

Fasten off, leaving a long tail. Use tail to join back seam, then bury tail through body of nigiri rice.

TAMAGO TOP

(make 2)

Using Yellow, ch6.

Round 1: Beg in 2nd ch from hook, 1dc in next 4 ch, 3dc in last ch, working down opp side of chain, 1dc in next 3 ch, 2dc in last ch. (12 sts)

Sl st in next st, PM to set new start of round and create rectangle.

Round 2: [1dc in next 3 sts, 3dc in next st, 1dc, 3dc in next st] twice. (20 sts)

Round 3: [1dc in next 4 sts, 3dc in next st, 1dc in next 3 sts, 3dc in next st, 1dc in next st] twice. (28 sts)

Round 4: [1dc in next 5 sts, 3dc in next st, 1dc in next 5 sts, 3dc in next st, 1dc in next 2 sts] twice. (36 sts)

Round 5: [1dc in next 6 sts, 3dc in next st, 1dc in next 7 sts, 3dc in next st, 1dc in next 3 sts] twice. (44 sts)

Fasten off, leaving an extra-long tail for sewing.

Hold two tamago top pieces with WS tog and join with a dc seam (see page 126), working through BLO in top piece.

BLACK BAND

Using Black, ch31.

Row 1: Beg in 2nd ch from hook, 1dc in next 29 ch, 3dc in last ch, cont down opp side of chain, 1dc in next 29 ch. (61 sts)

Fasten off, leaving a long tail for sewing.

Fold into loop and join two short ends.

MAKING UP AND FINISHING

Place Yellow piece on top of one nigiri rice and position Black band around centre, use a few small sts to secure as desired.

Fasten off and hide tail through body of tamago top.

SHRIMP NIGIRI (PICTURED RIGHT)

Make 1 Nigiri Rice (see opposite).

SHRIMP TOP

Note: Invisible increases and decreases are not used in this pattern.

Using Coral, ch4.

Row 1: Beg in 2nd ch from hook, 1dc in each ch. (*3 sts*)

Row 2: Ch1 (does not count as a st throughout), 1dc in each st.

Row 3: Ch1, 2dc in first st, 1dc in next st, 2dc in last st. (*5 sts*)

Row 4: Ch1, 1dc in each st.

Row 5: Ch1, 2dc in first st, 1dc in next 3 sts, 2dc in last st. (*7 sts*)

Rows 6–10: Ch1, 1dc in each st.

Row 11: Ch1, dc2tog, 1dc in next 3 sts, dc2tog. (*5 sts*)

Rows 12 and 13: Ch1, 1dc in each st.

Row 14: Ch1, 2dc in next st, 1dc in next 3 sts, 2dc in last st. (*7 sts*)

Rows 15–16: Ch1, 1dc in each st.

Row 17: Ch1, dc2tog, 1dc in next 3 sts, dc2tog. (*5 sts*)

Row 18: Ch1, 1dc in each st.

Row 19: Ch1, dc2tog, 1dc in next st, dc2tog. (*3 sts*)

Row 20: Ch1, 1dc in each st.

Fold in half and join one side edge with a dc seam.

Fasten off.

TAIL

Join yarn at short open end and working through both layers to close opening, (3tr, 1dtr, 3tr) in first st, sl st in next st (3tr, 1dtr, 3tr) in next st, do not turn.

Join with second side with a dc seam.

Fasten off.

MAKING UP AND FINISHING

Place Coral piece on top of second nigiri rice and use length of Light Pink yarn to secure in place with small sts on underside (see page 124). Add one long decorative stitch across top.

Fasten off and bury tail through body of shrimp top.

THREE PEAS IN A POD

This trio of cute little peas snuggle neatly together into a custom-sized pod. They are worked with two shades of green yarn for a lush finish.

SKILL RATING ● ○ ○

YARN AND MATERIALS

Cotton DK yarn (100% cotton)
    Light Green
    Dark Green
Three pairs of 5–6mm (⅜–¼in) safety eyes
Perlé Cotton No.8 in Black and Pink
Toy stuffing

HOOK AND EQUIPMENT

3.25mm (US size D/3) crochet hook
Locking or ring stitch marker
Yarn needle

FINISHED MEASUREMENTS

12.5 x 5cm (5 x 2in)

ABBREVIATIONS

See page 126

PEAS

(make 3)
Using Light Green, make a magic ring.
Round 1: 6dc into ring. (*6 sts*)
PM at start of round.
Round 2: [Inv inc in next st] 6 times. (*12 sts*)
Round 3: [1dc in next st, inv inc in next st] 6 times. (*18 sts*)
Round 4: [1dc in next 2 sts, inv inc in next st] 6 times. (*24 sts*)
Round 5: [1dc in next 3 sts, inv inc in next st] 6 times. (*30 sts*)
Weave in end from magic ring (see page 124).
Rounds 6–10: 1dc in each st.
Position safety eyes at centre front of each pea, evenly spaced, and fasten securely (see page 124). Sew face details using Perlé cotton and yarn needle, using Black for V-shaped mouth and Pink for cheeks (see page 125). Fasten off and secure all thread ends.
Round 11: [1dc in next 3 sts, inv dec] 6 times. (*24 sts*)
Beg filling with small pieces of toy stuffing, cont adding as dec rounds are worked.
Round 12: [1dc in next 2 sts, inv dec] 6 times. (*18 sts*)

Round 13: [1dc in next st, inv dec] 6 times. (*12 sts*)
Add final toy stuffing as needed.
Round 14: [Inv dec] 6 times. (*6 sts*)
Fasten off.
Cut yarn, thread tail into a yarn needle and close opening by weaving through front loops only. Fasten off and bury tail through body of pea.

POD

Using Dark Green, ch31.
Round 1: Beg in 2nd ch from hook, 1dc in next 29 ch, 2dc in last ch, cont down opp side of chain with 1dc in next 29 ch. (*60 sts*)
PM at start of round.
Round 2: Inv inc in first st, 1dc in next 28 sts, inv inc in next 2 sts, 1dc in next 28 sts, inv inc in next st. (*64 sts*)
Round 3: Inv inc in first st, 1dc in next 30 sts, inv inc in next 2 sts, 1dc in next 30 sts, inv inc in next st. (*68 sts*)
Round 4: Inv inc in first st, 1dc in next 32 sts, inv inc in next 2 sts, 1dc in next 32 sts, inv inc in next st. (*72 sts*)
Round 5: Inv inc in first st, 1dc in next 34 sts, inv inc in next 2 sts, 1dc in next 34 sts, inv inc in next st. (*76 sts*)

Round 6: Inv inc in first st, 1dc in next 36 sts, inv inc in next 2 sts, 1dc in next 36 sts, inv inc in next st. (*80 sts*)

Rounds 7 and 8: 1dc in each st.

Round 9: 1dc in next 12 sts, inv dec, 1dc in next 12 sts, inv dec, 1dc in next 24 sts, inv dec, 1dc in next 12 sts, inv dec, 1dc in next 12 sts. (*76 sts*)

Round 10: 1dc in next 10 sts, [inv dec] twice, 1dc in next 11 sts, [inv dec] twice, 1dc in next 18 sts, [inv dec] twice, 1dc in next 11 sts, [inv dec] twice, 1dc in next 10 sts. (*68 sts*)

Round 11: 1dc in next 9 sts, [inv dec] twice, 1dc in next 9 sts, [inv dec] twice, 1dc in next 16 sts, [inv dec] twice, 1dc in next 9 sts, [inv dec] twice, 1dc in next 9 sts. (*60 sts*)

Fasten off.

Cut yarn, weave in yarn end.

MAKING UP AND FINISHING

Weave in ends.

Place peas in pod.

PUMPKIN

Plump and ready for a harvest festival or Halloween, this bright orange pumpkin is finished with a chubby brown stalk, green leaves and a trailing stem.

SKILL RATING ● ● ●

YARN AND MATERIALS

Cotton DK yarn (100% cotton)
  Orange
  Brown
  Green
Pair of 5–6mm (⅜–¼in) safety eyes
Perlé Cotton No.8 in Black and White
Toy stuffing
Floristry or craft wire (15 gauge/1.5mm) (optional)

HOOK AND EQUIPMENT

3.25mm (US size D/3) crochet hook
Locking or ring stitch marker
Yarn needle

FINISHED MEASUREMENTS

10 x 6.5cm (4 x 2½in)

ABBREVIATIONS

See page 126

PUMPKIN

Using Orange, make a magic ring.
Round 1: 6dc into ring. (*6 sts*) PM at start of round.
Round 2: [Inv inc in next st] 6 times. (*12 sts*)
Round 3: [1dc in next st, inv inc in next st] 6 times. (*18 sts*)
Round 4: [1dc in next 2 sts, inv inc in next st] 6 times. (*24 sts*)
Round 5: [1dc in next 3 sts, inv inc in next st] 6 times. (*30 sts*)
Round 6: [1dc in next 4 sts, inv inc in next st] 6 times. (*36 sts*)
Round 7: [1dc in next 5 sts, inv inc in next st] 6 times. (*42 sts*)
Round 8: [1dc in next 6 sts, inv inc in next st] 6 times. (*48 sts*)
Round 9: [1dc in next 7 sts, inv inc in next st] 6 times. (*54 sts*)
Round 10: [1dc in next 8 sts, inv inc in next st] 6 times. (*60 sts*)
Rounds 11–21: 1dc in each st.
Round 22: [1dc in next 8 sts, inv dec] 6 times. (*54 sts*)
Position safety eyes at centre of a segment and fasten securely (see page 124).
Sew face details using Perlé cotton and yarn needle, using Black for V-shaped mouth and White for cheeks (see page 125). Fasten off and secure all thread ends.
Beg stuffing with small pieces of toy stuffing, cont adding as dec rounds are worked.

Round 23: [1dc in next 7 sts, inv dec] 6 times. (*48 sts*)
Round 24: [1dc in next 6 sts, inv dec] 6 times. (*42 sts*)
Round 25: [1dc in next 5 sts, inv dec] 6 times. (*36 sts*)
Round 26: [1dc in next 4 sts, inv dec] 6 times. (*30 sts*)
Round 27: [1dc in next 3 sts, inv dec] 6 times. (*24 sts*)
Round 28: [1dc in next 2 sts, inv dec] 6 times. (*18 sts*)
Round 29: [1dc in next st, inv dec] 6 times. (*12 sts*)
Add final toy stuffing as needed.
Round 30: [Inv dec] 6 times. (*6 sts*)
Fasten off.
Cut yarn, leaving an extra-long tail, thread tail into a yarn needle and close opening by weaving through front loops only.
Draw yarn from top through base of pumpkin, wrapping around outside of pumpkin and draw up to outline the segments.

STALK

Using Brown, make a magic ring.
Round 1: 6dc into ring. (*6 sts*) PM at start of round.
Rounds 2–5: 1dc in each st.
Round 6: [Inv inc in next st] 6 times. (*12 sts*)
Fasten off, leaving a long tail for sewing.

LEAF

Using Green, ch6.
Round 1: Sl st in 2nd ch from hook, 1dc in next ch, 1htr in next ch, 1tr in next ch, 8tr in last ch, cont down opp side of chain, 1tr in next ch, in next ch, 1dc in next ch, sl st in last ch.
Fasten off, leaving a long tail for sewing.

TRAILING STEM

Using Green, ch21.
Feed floristry wire through chain.
Fasten off, leaving a long tail for sewing.

MAKING UP AND FINISHING

Thread tail into a yarn needle and sew stalk onto centre top of pumpkin. Use tail to secure leaf and trailing stem into place; if using wire in stem, shape as desired. Fasten off and bury tail through body of pumpkin.

LEMON

Get zesty with this bright citrus fruit. The slightly elongated oval, worked in the boldest shade of yellow, is just round enough to give off plump, juicy vibes.

SKILL RATING ● ● ●

YARN AND MATERIALS

Cotton DK yarn (100% cotton)
   Bright Yellow
Pair of ⅜–¼in (5–6mm) safety eyes
Perlé Cotton No.8 in Black and Pink
Toy stuffing

HOOK AND EQUIPMENT

3.25mm (US size D/3) crochet hook
Locking or ring stitch marker
Yarn needle

FINISHED MEASUREMENTS

8.5 x 6cm (3¼ x 2¼in)

ABBREVIATIONS

See page 126

LEMON

Make a magic ring.
Round 1: 6dc into ring. (*6 sts*)
PM at start of round.
Round 2: [Inv inc in next st] 6 times. (*12 sts*)
Round 3: 1dc in each st.
Round 4: [1dc in next st, inv inc in next st] 6 times. (*18 sts*)
Round 5: [1dc in next 2 sts, inv inc in next st] 6 times. (*24 sts*)
Round 6: [1dc in next 3 sts, inv inc in next st] 6 times. (*30 sts*)
Round 7: [1dc in next 4 sts, inv inc in next st] 6 times. (*36 sts*)
Round 8: [1dc in next 5 sts, inv inc in next st] 6 times. (*42 sts*)
Weave in end from magic ring (see page 124).
Rounds 9–18: 1dc in each st.
Position safety eyes at centre front of lemon, evenly spaced, and fasten securely (see page 124).
Sew face details using Perlé cotton and yarn needle, using Black for V-shaped mouth and Pink for cheeks (see page 125). Fasten off and secure all thread ends.

Round 19: [1dc in next 5 sts, inv dec] 6 times. (*36 sts*)
Round 20: [1dc in next 4 sts, inv dec] 6 times. (*30 sts*)
Beg filling with small pieces of toy stuffing, cont adding as dec rounds are worked.
Round 21: [1dc in next 3 sts, inv dec] 6 times. (*24 sts*)
Round 22: [1dc in next 2 sts, inv dec] 6 times. (*18 sts*)
Round 23: [1dc in next st, inv dec] 6 times. (*12 sts*)
Rounds 24 and 25: 1dc in each st. Add final toy stuffing as needed.
Round 26: [Inv dec] 6 times. (*6 sts*)
Fasten off.

MAKING UP AND FINISHING

Cut yarn, thread tail into a yarn needle and close opening by weaving through front loops only. Fasten off and bury tail through body of lemon.

CHERRIES

These sweet cherries are a perfect pair. The bright red yarn for the fruit is teamed with a spring green for the stalk and leaf.

SKILL RATING ● ○ ○

YARN AND MATERIALS

Cotton DK yarn (100% cotton)
  Red
  Green
Pair of ⅜–¼in (5–6mm) safety eyes
Perlé Cotton No.8 in Black and White
Toy stuffing
Floristry or craft wire (15 gauge/1.5mm)

HOOK AND EQUIPMENT

3.25mm (US size D/3) crochet hook
Locking or ring stitch marker
Yarn needle

FINISHED MEASUREMENTS

10 x 8cm (4 x 3¼in)

ABBREVIATIONS

See page 126

CHERRIES

(make 2)
Using Red, make a magic ring.
Round 1: 6dc in ring. (*6 sts*)
PM at start of round.
Round 2: [Inv inc in next st] 6 times. (*12 sts*)
Round 3: [1dc in next st, inv inc in next st] 6 times. (*18 sts*)
Round 4: [1dc in next 2 sts, inv inc in next st] 6 times. (*24 sts*)
Round 5: [1dc in next 3 sts, inv inc in next st] 6 times. (*30 sts*)
Weave in end from magic ring (see page 124).
Rounds 6–10: 1dc in each st.
Position safety eyes at centre front of cherry and fasten securely (see page 124).
Sew face details using Perlé cotton and yarn needle, using Black for V-shaped mouth and White for cheeks (see page 125). Fasten off and secure all thread ends.
Round 11: [1dc in next 3 sts, inv dec] 6 times. (*24 sts*)
Beg filling with small pieces of toy stuffing, cont adding as dec rounds are worked.
Round 12: [1dc in next 2 sts, inv dec] 6 times. (*18 sts*)
Round 13: [1dc in next st, inv dec] 6 times. (*12 sts*)
Add final toy stuffing as needed.
Round 14: [Inv dec] 6 times. (*6 sts*)
Fasten off.

Cut yarn, thread tail into a yarn needle and close opening by weaving through front loops only. Fasten off and bury tail through body of cherry.

STALKS

(make 2)
Using Green, ch16.
Row 1: Beg in 2nd ch from hook, 1dc in each ch to end.
Fasten off, leaving a long tail tail for sewing.

LEAF

Using Green, ch6.
Row 1: 1sl st in 2nd ch from hook, 1dc in next ch, 1htr in next ch, 1tr in next ch, 8tr in last ch, cont down opp side of chain, 1tr in next ch, 1htr in next ch, 1dc in next ch, sl st in last ch.
Fasten off, leaving a long tail tail for sewing.

MAKING UP AND FINISHING

Feed length of floristry wire through stalk if desired. Ensure all ends of wire are folded in and wrapped tightly around itself.
Use tails to sew each stalk to cherries in turn. With tail from leaf, join stalks together and secure leaf in position.
Fasten off, weaving in all yarn ends (see page 124) and trimming.

CHAPTER 2

UNDERWATER ADVENTURES

CORAL REEF

Rippling coral and solid tubes create a fun reef design. With rust, blue and bright green yarn this coral captures the tones of the deep sea.

SKILL RATING ● ● ○

YARN AND MATERIALS
Cotton DK yarn (100% cotton)
    Rust
    Green
    Blue
Pair of 5–6mm (⅜–¼in) safety eyes
Perlé Cotton No.8 in Black and White
Toy stuffing

HOOK AND EQUIPMENT
3.25mm (US size D/3) crochet hook
Locking or ring stitch marker
Yarn needle

FINISHED MEASUREMENTS
10 x 10cm (4 x 4in)

ABBREVIATIONS
See page 126

CORAL REEF
Using Rust, ch7, join with sl st to form a ring.
Round 1: (1dc, 2htr, 16tr) in ring, do not join but cont working around in each st. (*19 sts*)
PM at start of round.
Rounds 2 and 3: 2tr in each st. (*38 sts*)
Round 4: 2tr in each st to last 5 sts, 1htr in next 2 sts, 1dc in next st, sl st in next 2 sts. (*71 sts*)
Round 5: Change to Green, 2dc in each st around. (*142 sts*)
Fasten off.

CORAL TUBE
Using Blue, make a magic ring.
Round 1: 6dc into ring. (*6 sts*)
PM at start of round.
Round 2: [Inv inc in next st] 6 times. (*12 sts*)
Round 3: [1dc in next st, inv inc in next st] 6 times. (*18 sts*)
Round 4: 1dcBLO in each st.
Rounds 5–16: 1dc in each st.

Position safety eyes at centre front of tube and fasten securely (see page 124).
Sew face details using Perlé cotton and yarn needle, using Black for V-shaped mouth and White for cheeks (see page 125). Fasten off and secure all thread ends.
Round 17: 1dcBLO in each st.
Beg filling with small pieces of toy stuffing, cont adding as dec rounds are worked.
Round 18: [1dc in next st, inv dec] 6 times. (*12 sts*)
Add final toy stuffing as needed.
Round 19: [Inv dec] 6 times. (*6 sts*)
Fasten off.
Cut yarn, thread tail into a yarn needle and close opening by weaving through front loops only. Fasten off and bury tail through body of coral tube.

HOLLOW TUBES

TUBE 1

Using Blue, make a magic ring.

Round 1: 6dc into ring. (*6 sts*)

PM at start of round.

Round 2: [Inv inc in next st]
6 times. (*12 sts*)

Round 3: 1dcBLO in each st.

Rounds 4–20: 1dc in each st.

Sl st in first st to join.

Fasten off and weave in end (see page 124).

TUBE 2

Using Blue, make a magic ring.

Round 1: 6dc into ring. (*6 sts*)

PM at start of round.

Round 2: [Inv inc in next st]
6 times. (*12 sts*)

Round 3: 1dcBLO in each st.

Rounds 4–24: 1dc in each st.

Sl st in first st to join.

Fasten off and weave in end.

MAKING UP AND FINISHING

Sew two hollow tubes tog, aligning bases. Align with coral tube and sew in place.

Sew bases of tubes into coral reef.

Fasten off and bury tail through body of coral reef.

JELLYFISH

A simple dome shape with curling tendrils makes for a very cute jellyfish, which is worked in shades of blues and green for a cool sea vibe.

SKILL RATING ● ● ◐

YARN AND MATERIALS
Cotton DK yarn (100% cotton)
  Light Blue
  Mint
  Marine Blue
Pair of 5–6mm (⅜–¼in) safety eyes
Perlé Cotton No.8 in Black and Pink
Toy stuffing

HOOK AND EQUIPMENT
3.25mm (US size D/3) crochet hook
Locking or ring stitch marker
Yarn needle

FINISHED MEASUREMENTS
8 x 19cm (3¼ x 7½in)

ABBREVIATIONS
See page 126

JELLYFISH HEAD
Using Light Blue, make a magic ring.
Round 1: 8dc into ring. (*8 sts*)
PM at start of round.
Round 2: [Inv inc in next st] 8 times. (*16 sts*)
Round 3: [1dc in next st, inv inc in next st] 8 times. (*24 sts*)
Round 4: [1dc in next 2 sts, inv inc in next st] 8 times. (*32 sts*)
Round 5: [1dc in next 3 sts, inv inc in next st] 8 times. (*40 sts*)
Round 6: [1dc in next 4 sts, inv inc in next st] 8 times. (*48 sts*)
Round 7: 1dc in each st.
Round 8: [1dc in next 5 sts, inv inc in next st] 8 times. (*56 sts*)
Rounds 9–15: 1dc in each st.
Position safety eyes at centre front of head and fasten securely (see page 124).
Sew face details using Perlé cotton and yarn needle, using Black for V-shaped mouth and Pink for cheeks (see page 125). Fasten off and secure all thread ends.
Round 16: [1dc in next st, inv dec] 4 times, [1dc in next 2 sts, inv dec] 8 times, [1dc in next st, inv dec] 4 times. (*40 sts*)
Fasten off.

BASE
Using Light Blue, make a magic ring.
Round 1: 8dc into ring. (*8 sts*)
PM at start of round.
Round 2: [Inv inc in next st] 8 times. (*16 sts*)
Round 3: 1dc in each st.
Round 4: [1dc in next st, inv inc in next st] 8 times. (*24 sts*)
Round 5: 1dc in each st.
Round 6: [1dc in next 2 sts, inv inc in next st] 8 times. (*32 sts*)
Round 7: 1dc in each st.
Round 8: [1dc in next 3 sts, inv inc in next st] 8 times. (*40 sts*)
Fasten off.

TENDRILS
(make 4 in Mint, 3 in Marine Blue)
Ch50.
Row 1: Beg in 2nd ch from hook, 2dc in each ch to end. (*98 sts*)
Fasten off, leaving a long tail for sewing.

MAKING UP AND FINISHING
Using tails of tendrils, secure to RS of base and knot securely.
Fill head with toy stuffing, working with small pieces at a time. Aligning sts, place head and base tog and join with a sl st seam around (see page 126). Add stuffing as necessary to ensure that Jellyfish is firmly stuffed before working last few sts. Fasten off and bury tail through body of the jellyfish.

AXOLOTL

Axolotls, also called Mexican Walking Fish, are as cute as can be with their cylindrical bodies, wide head and antennae. These are worked in two shades of pretty pink yarn.

SKILL RATING ● ● ○

YARN AND MATERIALS

Cotton DK yarn (100% cotton)
  Light Pink
  Dark Pink
Pair of 5–6mm (⅜–¼in) safety eyes
Perlé Cotton No.8 in Black and Pink
Toy stuffing

HOOK AND EQUIPMENT

3.25mm (US size D/3) crochet hook
Locking or ring stitch marker
Yarn needle
Pins

FINISHED MEASUREMENTS

12.5 x 15cm (5 x 6in)

ABBREVIATIONS

See page 126

HEAD

Using Light Pink, make a magic ring.
Round 1: 6dc into ring. (*6 sts*)
PM at start of round.
Round 2: [Inv inc in next st] 6 times. (*12 sts*)
Round 3: [1dc in next st, inv inc in next st] 6 times. (*18 sts*)
Round 4: [1dc in next 2 sts, inv inc in next st] 6 times. (*24 sts*)
Round 5: [1dc in next 3 sts, inv inc in next st] 6 times. (*30 sts*)
Round 6: [1dc in next 4 sts, inv inc in next st] 6 times. (*36 sts*)
Round 7: [1dc in next 5 sts, inv inc in next st] 6 times. (*42 sts*)
Round 8: [1dc in next 6 sts, inv inc in next st] 6 times. (*48 sts*)
Rounds 9–16: 1dc in each st.
Round 17: [1dc in next 6 sts, inv dec] 6 times. (*42 sts*)

Round 18: [1dc in next 5 sts, inv dec] 6 times. (*36 sts*)
Round 19: [1dc in next 4 sts, inv dec] 6 times. (*30 sts*)
Position safety eyes at centre of face and fasten securely (see page 124).
Sew face details using Perlé cotton and yarn needle, using Black for V-shaped mouth and Pink for cheeks (see page 125). Fasten off and secure all thread ends.
Round 20: [1dc in next 3 sts, inv dec] 6 times. (*24 sts*)
Round 21: [1dc in next 2 sts, inv dec] 6 times. (*18 sts*)
Beg filling with small pieces of toy stuffing.
Fasten off, leaving a long tail for sewing. Set aside.

BODY

Using Light Pink, make a magic ring.
Round 1: 6dc into ring. (*6 sts*)
PM at start of round.
Round 2: [Inv inc in next st] 6 times. (*12 sts*)
Rounds 3 and 4: 1dc in each st.
Round 5: [1dc in next st, inv inc in next st] 6 times. (*18 sts*)
Rounds 6 and 7: 1dc in each st.
Round 8: [1dc in next 2 sts, inv inc in next st] 6 times. (*24 sts*)
Rounds 9 and 10: 1dc in each st.
Round 11: [1dc in next 3 sts, inv inc in next st] 6 times. (*30 sts*)
Round 12: 1dc in each st.
Round 13: [1dc in next 4 sts, inv inc in next st] 6 times. (*36 sts*)
Round 14: 1dc in each st.
Round 15: [1dc in next 5 sts, inv inc in next st] 6 times. (*42 sts*)
Rounds 16–22: 1dc in each st.
Round 23: [1dc in next 5 sts, inv dec] 6 times. (*36 sts*)
Round 24: [1dc in next 4 sts, inv dec] 6 times. (*30 sts*)
Round 25: [1dc in next 3 sts, inv dec] 6 times. (*24 sts*)
Round 26: [1dc in next 2 sts, inv dec] 6 times. (*18 sts*)
Beg filling with small pieces of toy stuffing.
Fasten off and weave in end (see page 124).
Set aside.

LEGS

(make 4)
Using Light Pink, make a magic ring.
Round 1: 8dc into ring. (*8 sts*)
PM at start of round.
Rounds 2–4: 1dc in each st.
Fasten off, leaving a long tail for sewing.

ANTENNAE

(make 6)
Using Dark Pink, make a magic ring.
Round 1: 8dc into ring. (*8 sts*)
PM at start of round.
Rounds 2–10: 1dc in each st. (*8 sts*)
Fasten off, leaving a long tail for sewing.

MAKING UP AND FINISHING

Secure antennae onto sides of head, placing three on each side. Pin in place first to ensure they are aligned. Sew in place using tails, remove pins.
Pin legs in place on body and sew upper and lower legs in place using tails, ensuring they are level. Remove pins.
Position head on top of body, aligning sts, working tail through one st on head and one st on body to join all around. Add stuffing as necessary to ensure that axolotl is firmly stuffed before securing last few sts.
Fasten off and bury tail through body of axolotl.

SEAHORSE

With a precious little snout and contrasting mane and fins, this little seahorse is a friendly character.

SKILL RATING ● ● ○

YARN AND MATERIALS

Cotton DK yarn (100% cotton)
  Mint
  Purple

Pair of 5–6mm (⅜–¼in) safety eyes

Perlé Cotton No.8 in Pink

Toy stuffing

Floristry or craft wire (15 gauge/1.5mm) (optional)

HOOK AND EQUIPMENT

3.25mm (US size D/3) crochet hook

Locking or ring stitch marker

Yarn needle

FINISHED MEASUREMENTS

7.5 x 15cm (3 x 6in)

ABBREVIATIONS

See page 126

SNOUT

Using Mint, make a magic ring.

Round 1: 8dc into ring. (*8 sts*)
PM at start of round.

Round 2: 1dcBLO in each st.

Round 3: 1dc in each st.
Fasten off, leaving a long tail for sewing.

HEAD

Using Mint, make a magic ring.

Round 1: 6dc into ring. (*6 sts*)
PM at start of round.

Round 2: [Inv inc in next st] 6 times. (*12 sts*)

Round 3: [1dc in next st, inv inc in next st] 6 times. (*18 sts*)

Round 4: [1dc in next 2 sts, inv inc in next st] 6 times. (*24 sts*)

Round 5: [1dc in next 3 sts, inv inc in next st] 6 times. (*30 sts*)
Weave in end from magic ring (see page 124).

Round 6: [1dc in next 4 sts, inv inc in next st] 6 times. (*36 sts*)

Rounds 7–13: 1dc in each st.

Position snout at centre front of face, sew in place using yarn tail and yarn needle.

Position safety eyes at centre front of face, evenly spaced, and fasten securely (see page 124).

Sew cheek details using Pink Perlé cotton and yarn needle (seep page 125). Fasten off and secure all thread ends.

Round 14: [1dc in next 4 sts, inv dec] 6 times. (*30 sts*)

Round 15: [1dc in next 3 sts, inv dec] 6 times. (*24 sts*)

Beg filling with small pieces of toy stuffing, cont adding as dec rounds are worked.

Round 16: [1dc in next 2 sts, inv dec] 6 times. (*18 sts*)

Round 17: [1dc in next st, inv dec] 6 times. (*12 sts*)

BODY

Round 18: [1dc in next st, inv inc in next st] 6 times. (*18 sts*)

Round 19: [1dc in next 2 sts, inv inc in next st] 6 times. (*24 sts*)

Round 20: 1dc in next 9 sts, inv inc in next st, [1dc in next 2 sts, inv inc in next st] twice, 1dc in next 8 sts. (*27 sts*)

Cont adding toy stuffing as inc rounds are worked.

Round 21: 1dc in next 10 sts, 1htr in next st, 1dc in next 2 sts, 1htr in next 2 sts, 1dc in next 2 sts, 1htr in next st, 1dc in next 9 sts.

Round 22: 1dc in next 10 sts, inv inc in next st, 1dc in next 2 sts, inv inc in next st, 1dc in next 3 sts, inv inc in next st, 1dc in next 9 sts. (*30 sts*)

Rounds 23–27: 1dc in each st.

Round 28: [1dc in next 3 sts, inv dec] 6 times. (*24 sts*)

Round 29: [1dc in next 2 sts, inv dec] 6 times. (*18 sts*)

Rounds 30–32: 1dc in each st.

Round 33: [1dc in next st, inv dec] 6 times. (*12 sts*)

(Optional: Insert folded length of floristry wire long enough to run from head to tail.)

Rounds 34–43: 1dc in each st.

Round 44: [1dc in next 2 sts, inv dec] 3 times. (*9 sts*)

Rounds 45–50: 1dc in each st.

Round 51: [1dc in next st, inv dec] 3 times. (*6 sts*)

Add final toy stuffing as needed.

Rounds 52–56: 1dc in each st.

Cut yarn, leaving a long tail for sewing, thread tail into a yarn needle and close opening by weaving through front loops only. Fasten off.

MANE

Using Purple, ch20.

Row 1: Beg in 2nd ch from hook, 1dc in each ch to end. (*19 sts*)

Row 2: 6htr in first st, skip 1 st, sl st in next st, [skip 1 st, 6htr in next st, skip 1 st, sl st in next st] 4 times.

Fasten off, leaving a long tail for sewing.

FINS

(make 2)

Using Purple, make a magic ring.

Round 1: 8dc into ring. (*8 sts*)

PM at start of round.

Round 2: 1dc in next 2 sts, 3htr in next 3 sts, 1dc in next 2 sts, sl st in next st.

Fasten off, leaving a long tail for sewing.

MAKING UP AND FINISHING

Place mane onto crown of head, secure in place down back section using yarn tail.

Place a fin on each side of the body and secure into place using yarn tails.

If using floristry wire inside tail, shape into desired position. Roll up end of tail and secure in place using yarn tail.

Fasten off and bury all tails.

CRAB

This snappy little chappie has two large claws
and is a cute creature from the deep.

SKILL RATING ● ● ○

YARN AND MATERIALS

Cotton DK yarn (100% cotton)
  Red
  White
  Peach
Pair of 5–6mm (⅜–¼in) safety eyes
Perlé Cotton No.8 in Pink and Black
Toy stuffing
Mylar® or piece of fairly stiff plastic
(optional)

HOOK AND EQUIPMENT

3.25mm (US size D/3) crochet hook
Locking or ring stitch marker
Yarn needle

FINISHED MEASUREMENTS

7.5 x 12.5cm (3 x 5in)

ABBREVIATIONS

See page 126

EYES

(make 2)
Using Red, make a magic ring.
Round 1: 6dc into ring. (*6 sts*)
PM at start of round.
Round 2: [Inv inc in next st] 6 times.
(*12 sts*)
Rounds 3–5: 1dc in each st.
Fasten off, leaving a long tail
for sewing.

EYE ACCENTS

(make 2)

Using White, make a magic ring.

Round 1: 6dc into ring, sl st in first st to join. (*6 sts*)

Fasten off, leaving a long tail for sewing.

Position safety eye at centre of each eye accent and fasten securely (see page 124).

Place eye accent onto front of each Red eye and use yarn tail to secure into place. Set aside.

HEAD

Using Red, make a magic ring.

Round 1: 8dc into ring. (*8 sts*)

PM at start of round.

Round 2: [Inv inc in next st] 8 times. (*16 sts*)

Round 3: [1dc in next st, inv inc in next st] 8 times. (*24 sts*)

Round 4: [1dc in next 2 sts, inv inc in next st] 8 times. (*32 sts*)

Round 5: [1dc in next 3 sts, inv inc in next st] 8 times. (*40 sts*)

Weave in end from magic ring (see page 124).

Round 6: [1dc in next 4 sts, inv inc in next st] 8 times. (*48 sts*)

Round 7: [1dc in next 5 sts, inv inc in next st] 8 times. (*56 sts*)

Rounds 8–13: 1dc in each st.

Round 14: [1dc in next 5 sts, inv dec] 8 times. (*48 sts*)

Fasten off, leaving a long tail for sewing.

Place eyes onto top of head, evenly spaced, using yarn tails to secure each eye in turn.

Sew face details using Perlé cotton and yarn needle, using Pink for cheeks and Black for V-shaped mouth (see page 125). Fasten off and secure all thread ends.

TUMMY

Using Peach, make a magic ring.

Round 1: 8dc into ring. (*8 sts*)

PM at start of round.

Round 2: [Inv inc in next st] 8 times. (*16 sts*)

Round 3: [1dc in next st, inv inc in next st] 8 times. (*24 sts*)

Round 4: [1dc in next 2 sts, inv inc in next st] 8 times. (*32 sts*)

Round 5: [1dc in next 3 sts, inv inc in next st] 8 times. (*40 sts*)

Weave in end from magic ring.

Round 6: [1dc in next 4 sts, inv inc in next st] 8 times. (*48 sts*)

Round 7: [1dc in next 5 sts, inv inc in next st] 8 times. (*56 sts*)

Fasten off, leaving a long tail for sewing.

LEGS

(make 8)

Using Red, make a magic ring.

Round 1: 6dc into ring. (*6 sts*)

PM at start of round.

Round 2: 1dc in each st.

Rounds 3–6: 1htr in next 3 sts, 1dc in next 3 sts.

Fasten off, leaving a long tail for sewing.

CLAWS

(make 2)

First claw piece

Using Red, make a magic ring.

Round 1: 6dc into ring. (*6 sts*)

PM at start of round.

Rounds 2 and 3: 1dc in each st.

Fasten off and set aside.

Second claw piece

Using Red, make a magic ring.

Round 1: 6dc into ring. (*6 sts*)

PM at start of round.

Round 2: 1dc in each st.

Round 3: [1dc in next st, inv inc in next st] 3 times. (*9 sts*)

Round 4: [1dc in next 2 sts, inv inc in next st] 3 times. (*12 sts*)

JOIN CLAW PIECES

Round 5: Place first claw piece next to second piece, 1dc in each of 6 sts around first claw piece, 1dc in each of 12 sts around second claw piece. (*18 sts*)

Rounds 6 and 7: 1dc in each st.

Round 8: [1dc in next st, inv dec] 6 times. (*12 sts*)

Round 9: [Inv dec] 6 times. (*6 sts*)

Fasten off, leaving a long tail for sewing.

MAKING UP AND FINISHING

Place tummy section onto head, using yarn tail begin to join pieces together working through inside loops only.

(Optional: Cut circular piece of Mylar® or fairly stiff plastic and place into base to fit neatly on tummy section.)

Begin stuffing. Before sealing up completely ensure body is fully stuffed. Fasten off.

Working on each side in turn, using yarn tails, sew four legs and one claw to each side.

Fasten off and bury all tails.

SAILOR

Raise the anchor and get all shipshape to sail the seven seas with this jolly sailor.

SKILL RATING ● ● ●

YARN AND MATERIALS

Cotton DK yarn (100% cotton)
  Light Pink
  Orange
  Black
  Blue
  Red
  White
  Gold
  Yellow
Pair of 5–6mm (⅜–¼in) safety eyes
Perlé Cotton No.8 in Pink
Toy stuffing

HOOK AND EQUIPMENT

3.25mm (US size D/3) crochet hook
Locking or ring stitch marker
Yarn needle
Pins

FINISHED MEASUREMENTS

10 x 17.5cm (4 x 7in)

ABBREVIATIONS

See page 126

HEAD

Using Light Pink, make a magic ring.
Round 1: 6dc into ring. (*6 sts*)
PM at start of round.
Round 2: [Inv inc in next st] 6 times. (*12 sts*)
Round 3: [1dc in next st, inv inc in next st] 6 times. (*18 sts*)
Round 4: [1dc in next 2 sts, inv inc in next st] 6 times. (*24 sts*)
Round 5: [1dc in next 3 sts, inv inc in next st] 6 times. (*30 sts*)
Round 6: [1dc in next 4 sts, inv inc in next st] 6 times. (*36 sts*)
Round 7: [1dc in next 5 sts, inv inc in next st] 6 times. (*42 sts*)
Round 8: [1dc in next 6 sts, inv inc in next st] 6 times. (*48 sts*)
Weave in end from magic ring (see page 124).
Rounds 9–17: 1dc in each st.
Position safety eyes at centre front of face, evenly spaced, and fasten securely (see page 124).
Sew cheek details using Pink Perlé cotton and yarn needle (see page 125). Fasten off and secure all thread ends.
Round 18: [1dc in next 6 sts, inv dec] 6 times. (*42 sts*)
Round 19: [1dc in next 5 sts, inv dec] 6 times. (*36 sts*)
Round 20: [1dc in next 4 sts, inv dec] 6 times. (*30 sts*)
Beg filling with small pieces of toy stuffing, cont adding as dec rounds are worked.
Round 21: [1dc in next 3 sts, inv dec] 6 times. (*24 sts*)
Round 22: [1dc in next 2 sts, inv dec] 6 times. (*18 sts*)
Add final toy stuffing as needed.
Round 23: [1dc in next st, inv dec] 6 times. (*12 sts*)
Fasten off, leaving a long tail for sewing.

HAIR

Using Orange, make a magic ring.
Round 1: 6dc into ring. (*6 sts*)
PM at start of round.
Round 2: [Inv inc in next st] 6 times. (*12 sts*)
Round 3: [1dc in next st, inv inc in next st] 6 times. (*18 sts*)
Round 4: [1dc in next 2 sts, inv inc in next st] 6 times. (*24 sts*)
Round 5: [1dc in next 3 sts, inv inc in next st] 6 times. (*30 sts*)
Round 6: [1dc in next 4 sts, inv inc in next st] 6 times. (*36 sts*)
Round 7: [1dc in next 5 sts, inv inc in next st] 6 times. (*42 sts*)
Round 8: [1dc in next 6 sts, inv inc in next st] 6 times. (*48 sts*)
Rounds 9–15: 1dc in each st.
Round 16: 1dcBLO in next 16 sts, 1htrBLO in next 2 sts, 1trBLO in next 3 sts, working in both loops, sl st in next st, 1trBLO in next 3 sts, 1htrBLO in next 2 sts, 1dcBLO in next 21 sts. Fasten off, leaving a long tail for sewing.

JOIN LEGS

Round 11: Place first leg next to second leg, 1dc in each of 18 sts around first leg, 1dc in each of 18 sts around second leg. (*36 sts*)

BODY

Rounds 12 and 13: 1dc in each st.

Round 14: Change to Black, 1dcBLO in each st.

Round 15: Change to Red, 1dcBLO in each st.

Round 16: 1dc in each st.

Round 17: Change to White, 1dc in each st.

Beg filling with small pieces of toy stuffing, cont adding as dec rounds are worked.

Round 18: [1dc in next 4 sts, inv dec] 6 times. (*30 sts*)

Rounds 19 and 20: Change to Red, 1dc in each st.

Round 21: Change to White, [1dc in next 3 sts, inv dec] 6 times. (*24 sts*)

Round 22: 1dc in each st.

Round 23: Change to Red, [1dc in next 2 sts, inv dec] 6 times. (*18 sts*)
Add final toy stuffing as needed.

Round 24: [1dc in next st, inv dec] 6 times. (*12 sts*)

Fasten off, leaving a long tail for sewing.

ARMS

(make 2)

Using Light Pink, make a magic ring.

Round 1: 6dc into ring. (*6 sts*)
PM at start of round.

Round 2: [Inv inc in next st] 6 times. (*12 sts*)

Round 3: 1dc in each st.

Round 4: 1dc in next 10 sts, inv dec. (*11 sts*)

Round 5: 1dc in next 9 sts, inv dec. (*10 sts*)

Rounds 6 and 7: 1dc in each st.

Rounds 8 and 9: Change to Red, 1dc in each st.

FIRST LEG

Using Black, make a magic ring.

Round 1: 6dc into ring. (*6 sts*)
PM at start of round.

Round 2: [1dc in next st, inv inc in next st] 3 times. (*9 sts*)

Round 3: 1dc in each st.

Round 4: Change to Light Pink, [1dc in next 2 sts, inv inc in next st] 3 times. (*12 sts*)

Rounds 5–8: 1dc in each st.
Weave in end from magic ring.

Round 9: Change to Blue, [1dc in next st, inv inc in next st] 6 times. (*18 sts*)

Round 10: 1dc in each st.
Fasten off first leg, set aside.

SECOND LEG

Using Black, make a magic ring.

Round 1: 6dc into ring. (*6 sts*)
PM at start of round.

Round 2: [1dc in next st, inv inc in next st] 3 times. (*9 sts*)

Round 3: 1dc in each st.

Round 4: Change to Light Pink, [1dc in next 2 sts, inv inc in next st] 3 times. (*12 sts*)

Rounds 5–8: 1dc in each st.
Weave in end from magic ring.

Round 9: Change to Blue, [1dc in next st, inv inc in next st] 6 times. (*18 sts*)

Round 10: 1dc in each st.
Do not fasten off.

Rounds 10 and 11: Change to White, 1dc in each st.

Rounds 12 and 13: Change to Red, 1dc in each st.

Rounds 14 and 15: Change to White, 1dc in each st.

Rounds 16 and 17: Change to Red, 1dc in each st.

Fasten off, leaving a long tail for sewing.

BEARD

Using Orange, make a magic ring.

Round 1: 6dc into ring. (*6 sts*) PM at start of round.

Round 2: 1dc in each st.

Round 3: [Inv inc in next st] 6 times. (*12 sts*)

Round 4: [1dc in next st, inv inc in next st] 6 times. (*18 sts*)

Round 5: 1dc in each st.

Round 6: [1dc in next 2 sts, inv inc in next st] 6 times. (*24 sts*)

Round 7: [1dc in next 3 sts, inv inc in next st] 6 times. (*30 sts*)

Round 8: [1dc in next 4 sts, inv inc in next st] 6 times. (*36 sts*)

Round 9: [1dc in next 5 sts, inv inc in next st] 6 times. (*42 sts*)

Round 10: [1dc in next 6 sts, inv inc in next st] 6 times. (*48 sts*)

Round 11: [1dc in next 7 sts, inv inc in next st] 6 times. (*54 sts*)

Round 12: [1dc in next 8 sts, inv inc in next st] 6 times. (*60 sts*)

Fold in half, work through BLO to join front and back tog.

Round 13: 1dcBLO in next 9 sts, 1htrBLO in next 2 sts, 1trBLO in next 3 sts, working in both loops, sl st in next 2 sts, 1trBLO in next 3 sts, 1htrBLO in next 2 sts, 1dcBLO in next 9 sts.

Fasten off, leaving a long tail for sewing.

HAT

Using Yellow, make a magic ring.

Round 1: 8dc into ring. (*8 sts*) PM at start of round.

Round 2: [Inv inc in next st] 8 times. (*16 sts*)

Round 3: [1dc in next st, inv inc in next st] 8 times. (*24 sts*)

Round 4: [1dc in next 2 sts, inv inc in next st] 8 times. (*32 sts*)

Round 5: [1dc in next 3 sts, inv inc in next st] 8 times. (*40 sts*)

Round 6: [1dc in next 4 sts, inv inc in next st] 8 times. (*48 sts*)

Rounds 7–9: 1dc in each st.

Rounds 10 and 11: 1htr in each st.

Fasten off, leaving a long tail for sewing.

BOBBLE

Using Yellow, make a magic ring.

Round 1: 6dc into ring. (*6 sts*) PM at start of round.

Round 2: 1dc in each st.

Round 3: [Inv inc in next st] 6 times. (*12 sts*)

Rounds 4–6: 1dc in each st.

Round 7: [Inv dec] 6 times. (*6 sts*)

Fasten off, leaving a long tail for sewing.

MAKING UP AND FINISHING

Place hair on top of head, positioning it to frame face, rotate to align hair line shaping with eyes. Use yarn tail to sew in place (see page 124).

Place beard onto front of face and use yarn tail to sew in place. With a short length of Gold and a yarn needle, work a small buckle detail on front of Black band around body using straight stitches. Fasten off.

Position bobble on top of hat and secure in place using yarn tail. Place hat on top of head and use yarn tail to secure in place.

Stuff arms lightly and pin onto sides of body. Place head onto body and sew in place using yarn tail, working through stitches around neck section. While working around ensure that upper sections of arms are secured into seam. Before working final stitches add in any additional toy stuffing to neck section to prevent it becoming floppy. Fasten off and bury all tails.

MERMAID

This lovely mermaid is a true siren of the sea, with her layers of luscious curling locks.

HAIR PIECE 1

Using Hot Pink, make a magic ring.
Round 1: 6dc into ring. (*6 sts*)
PM at start of round.
Round 2: [Inv inc in next st] 6 times. (*12 sts*)
Round 3: [Sl st in next st, ch3, beg in 2nd ch from hook, 1htr in next 12 ch, skip next st, sl st in next st] 4 times.
Fasten off, leaving a long tail for sewing.

HAIR PIECE 2

Using Hot Pink, make a magic ring.
Round 1: 6dc into ring. (*6 sts*)
PM at start of round.
Round 2: [Inv inc in next st] 6 times. (*12 sts*)
Round 3: [1dc in next st, inv inc in next st] 6 times. (*18 sts*)
Round 4: [1dc in next 2 sts, inv inc in next st] 6 times. (*24 sts*)
Round 5: [Sl st in next st, ch25, beg in 2nd ch from hook, 1htr in next 24 ch, skip next st, sl st in next st] 8 times.
Fasten off, leaving a long tail for sewing.

HAIR PIECE 3

Using Hot Pink, make a magic ring.
Round 1: 6dc into ring. (*6 sts*)
PM at start of round.
Round 2: [Inv inc in next st] 6 times. (*12 sts*)
Round 3: [1dc in next st, inv inc in next st] 6 times. (*18 sts*)

Round 4: [1dc in next 2 sts, inv inc in next st] 6 times. (*24 sts*)
Round 5: [1dc in next 3 sts, inv inc in next st] 6 times. (*30 sts*)
Round 6: [1dc in next 4 sts, inv inc in next st] 6 times. (*36 sts*)
Round 7: [Sl st in next st, ch31, beg in 2nd ch from hook, 1htr in next 30 ch, skip next st, sl st in next st] twice.
Fasten off, leaving a long tail for sewing.

HAIR PIECE 4

Using Hot Pink, ch34.
Round 1: Beg in 2nd ch from hook, 1dc in each ch to end. (*33 sts*)
Round 2: [Sl st in next st, ch37, beg in 2nd ch from hook, 1htr in next 36 ch, skip next st, sl st in next st] 11 times.
Fasten off, leaving a long tail for sewing.

HAIR ACCENT

Using Dark Aqua, make a magic ring.
Round 1: 5dc into ring. (*5 sts*)
PM at start of round.
Round 2: Sl st in first st, [ch3, beg in 2nd ch from hook, 1dc in next 2 ch, sl st in next st] 4 times.
Fasten off, leaving a long tail for sewing.

HEAD

Using Light Pink, make a magic ring.
Round 1: 6dc into ring. (*6 sts*)
PM at start of round.
Round 2: [Inv inc in next st] 6 times. (*12 sts*)
Round 3: [1dc in next st, inv inc in next st] 6 times. (*18 sts*)
Round 4: [1dc in next 2 sts, inv inc in next st] 6 times. (*24 sts*)
Round 5: [1dc in next 3 sts, inv inc in next st] 6 times. (*30 sts*)
Round 6: [1dc in next 4 sts, inv inc in next st] 6 times. (*36 sts*)
Round 7: [1dc in next 5 sts, inv inc in next st] 6 times. (*42 sts*)
Round 8: [1dc in next 6 sts, inv inc in next st] 6 times. (*48 sts*)
Weave in end from magic ring (see page 124).
Rounds 9–17: 1dc in each st.

Position safety eyes at centre front of face, evenly spaced, and fasten securely (see page 124). Sew face details using Perlé cotton and yarn needle, using Pink for cheeks and Black for V-shaped mouth (see page 125). Fasten off and secure all thread ends.
Round 18: [1dc in next 6 sts, inv dec] 6 times. (*42 sts*)
Round 19: [1dc in next 5 sts, inv dec] 6 times. (*36 sts*)
Layer hair pieces 1, 2 and 3, using yarn tails to secure to crown of head, then wrap hair piece 4 around back of head and sew in place before stuffing.
Round 20: [1dc in next 4 sts, inv dec] 6 times. (*30 sts*)

Beg filling with small pieces of toy stuffing, cont adding as dec rounds are worked.
Round 21: [1dc in next 3 sts, inv dec] 6 times. (*24 sts*)
Round 22: [1dc in next 2 sts, inv dec] 6 times. (*18 sts*)
Add final toy stuffing as needed.
Round 23: [1dc in next st, inv dec] 6 times. (*12 sts*)
Fasten off, leaving a long tail for sewing.

TAIL

Using Dark Aqua, make a magic ring.
Round 1: 6dc into ring. (*6 sts*)
PM at start of round.
Rounds 2 and 3: 1dc in each st.
Round 4: [1dc in next st, inv inc in next st] 3 times. (*9 sts*)
Rounds 5 and 6: 1dc in each st.
Round 7: [1dc in next 2 sts, inv inc in next st] 3 times. (*12 sts*)
Rounds 8 and 9: 1dc in each st.
Round 10: [1dc in next 3 sts, inv inc in next st] 3 times. (*15 sts*)
Rounds 11 and 12: 1dc in each st.
Round 13: [1dc in next 4 sts, inv inc in next st] 3 times. (*18 sts*)
Rounds 14 and 15: 1dc in each st.
Round 16: [1dc in next 5 sts, inv inc in next st] 3 times. (*21 sts*)
Rounds 17 and 18: 1dc in each st.
Round 19: [1dc in next 6 sts, inv inc in next st] 3 times. (*24 sts*)
Rounds 20–22: 1dc in each st.
Round 23: [1dc in next 7 sts, inv inc in next st] 3 times. (*27 sts*)
Rounds 24–27: 1dc in each st.
Round 28: [1dc in next 8 sts, inv inc in next st] 3 times. (*30 sts*)
Rounds 29–32: 1dc in each st.
Round 33: [1dc in next 9 sts, inv inc in next st] 3 times. (*33 sts*)
Rounds 34–37: 1dc in each st.
Round 38: [1dc in next 10 sts, inv inc in next st] 3 times. (*36 sts*)

BODY

Rounds 39–42: 1dc in each st. (Optional: Insert a folded section of floristry wire to run length of tail piece now.)

Round 43: [1dc in next 4 sts, inv dec] 6 times. (*30 sts*)

Beg filling with small pieces of toy stuffing, cont adding as dec rounds are worked.

Rounds 44 and 45: 1dc in each st.

Rounds 46: Change to Light Pink, 1dcBLO in each st.

Round 47: [1dc in next 3 sts, inv dec] 6 times. (*24 sts*)

Round 48: 1dc in each st.

Round 49: [1dc in next 2 sts, inv dec] 6 times. (*18 sts*)

Add final toy stuffing as needed.

Round 50: [1dc in next st, inv dec] 6 times. (*12 sts*)

Fasten off, leaving a long tail for sewing.

TAIL ACCENT

Round 1: Join Light Aqua to unworked FLO of Dark Aqua at colour change between tail and body and work 1dc in each of next 30 sts.

Round 2: [Sl st in next st, 3htr in next st, sl st in next st] 10 times. Fasten off.

FINS

(make 2)

Using Light Aqua, make a magic ring.

Round 1: 4dc into ring. (*4 sts*) PM at start of round.

Round 2: [1dc in next st, inv inc in next st] twice. (*6 sts*)

Round 3: [1dc in next st, inv inc in next st] 3 times. (*9 sts*)

Round 4: [1dc in next 2 sts, inv inc in next st] 3 times. (*12 sts*)

Round 5: [1dc in next 3 sts, inv inc in next st] 3 times. (*15 sts*)

Round 6: [1dc in next 4 sts, inv inc in next st] 3 times. (*18 sts*)

Rounds 7–10: 1dc in each st.

Round 11: [1dc in next st, inv dec] 6 times. (*12 sts*)

Round 12: [1dc in next st, inv dec] 4 times. (*8 sts*)

Round 13: [Inv dec] 4 times. (*4 sts*)

Fasten off, leaving a long tail for sewing.

ARMS

(make 2)

Using Light Pink, make a magic ring.

Round 1: 6dc into ring. (*6 sts*) PM at start of round.

Round 2: [Inv inc in next st] 6 times. (*12 sts*)

Round 3: 1dc in each st.

Round 4: 1dc in next 10 sts, inv dec. (*11 sts*)

Round 5: 1dc in next 9 sts, inv dec. (*10 sts*)

Rounds 6–17: 1dc in each st. Fasten off, leaving a long tail for sewing.

SHELL BIKINI

Using Mid Pink, ch6.

Row 1: (2htr, 1tr, 2htr) in 2nd ch from hook, skip next ch, (2htr, 1tr, 2htr) in next ch, skip next ch, sl st in last ch. Fasten off, leaving a long tail for sewing.

MAKING UP AND FINISHING

Stuff arms lightly and pin onto sides of body. Place head onto body, using yarn tail and working through stitches around neck section, sew in place (see page 124). While working around ensure that upper sections of arms are secured into seam. Before working final stitches add in any additional toy stuffing to neck section to prevent it becoming floppy.

Place fins on either side of tail and use yarn tails to sew place. If using floristry wire inside tail, shape into desired position.

Place hair accent onto head and secure using yarn tail.

Position shell bikini onto front of body and sew into place using yarn tail. Fasten off and bury all tails.

CHAPTER 3

OUT IN THE GARDEN

BUNNY

A sweet bunny is all set for the day in her blue dungarees. Her large, floppy ears are the perfect finishing touch.

SKILL RATING ● ● ●

YARN AND MATERIALS

Cotton DK yarn (100% cotton)
   Champagne White
   Denim Blue
Pair of 5–6mm (⅜–¼in) safety eyes
Perlé Cotton No.8 in Black and Pink
Toy stuffing

HOOK AND EQUIPMENT

3.25mm (US size D/3) crochet hook
Locking or ring stitch marker
Yarn needle
Pins

FINISHED MEASUREMENTS

9.5 x 15cm (3¾ x 15cm),
20cm (8in) tall with ears extended

ABBREVIATIONS

See page 126

HEAD

Using Champagne White, make a magic ring.
Round 1: 6dc into ring. (*6 sts*)
PM at start of round.
Round 2: [Inv inc in next st] 6 times. (*12 sts*)
Round 3: [1dc in next st, inv inc in next st] 6 times. (*18 sts*)
Round 4: [1dc in next 2 sts, inv inc in next st] 6 times. (*24 sts*)
Round 5: [1dc in next 3 sts, inv inc in next st] 6 times. (*30 sts*)
Weave in end from magic ring (see page 124).
Round 6: [1dc in next 4 sts, inv inc in next st] 6 times. (*36 sts*)
Round 7: [1dc in next 5 sts, inv inc in next st] 6 times. (*42 sts*)
Round 8: [1dc in next 6 sts, inv inc in next st] 6 times. (*48 sts*)
Rounds 9–17: 1dc in each st.
Round 18: [1dc in next 6 sts, inv dec] 6 times. (*42 sts*)
Round 19: [1dc in next 5 sts, inv dec] 6 times. (*36 sts*)
Round 20: [1dc in next 4 sts, inv dec] 6 times. (*30 sts*)
Round 21: [1dc in next 3 sts, inv dec] 6 times. (*24 sts*)

Position safety eyes at centre front of head, evenly spaced, and fasten securely (see page 124).
Sew face details using Perlé cotton and yarn needle, using Black for V-shaped mouth and Pink for cheeks (see page 125). Fasten off and secure all thread ends.
Round 22: [1dc in next 2 sts, inv dec] 6 times. (*18 sts*)
Round 23: [1dc in next st, inv dec] 6 times. (*12 sts*)
Fasten off, leaving a long tail for sewing.

ARMS

(make 2)
Using Champagne White, make a magic ring.
Round 1: 6dc into ring. (*6 sts*)
PM at start of round.
Round 2: [Inv inc in next st] 6 times. (*12 sts*)
Round 3: 1dc in each st.
Round 4: 1dc in next 10 sts, inv dec. (*11 sts*)
Round 5: 1dc in next 9 sts, inv dec. (*10 sts*)
Weave in end from magic ring.
Rounds 6–17: 1dc in each st.
Fasten off, leaving a long tail for sewing.

BODY

Worked from legs upwards.

FIRST LEG

Using Champagne White, make a magic ring.

Round 1: 6dc into ring. (*6 sts*) PM at start of round.

Round 2: [Inv inc in next st] 6 times. (*12 sts*)

Round 3: [1dc in next st, inv inc in next st] 6 times. (*18 sts*)

Rounds 4–6: 1dc in each st. Fasten off Champagne White, change to Denim Blue.

Rounds 7 and 8: 1dc in each st. Fasten off first leg, set aside.

SECOND LEG

Using Champagne White, make a magic ring.

Round 1: 6dc into ring. (*6 sts*) PM at start of round.

Round 2: [Inv inc in next st] 6 times. (*12 sts*)

Round 3: [1dc in next st, inv inc in next st] 6 times. (*18 sts*)

Rounds 4–6: 1dc in each st. Fasten off Champagne White, change to Denim Blue.

Rounds 7 and 8: 1dc in each st.

Round 9: Place first leg next to second leg, work 18dc across first leg, then cont with 1dc in each st around second leg. (*36 sts*)

BODY

Rounds 10–16: 1dc in each st.

Round 17: [1dc in next 4 sts, inv dec] 6 times. (*30 sts*)

Rounds 18 and 19: 1dc in each st.

Round 20: [1dc in next 3 sts, inv dec] 6 times. (*24 sts*) Fasten off Denim Blue, change to Champagne White.

Round 21: 1dc in each st.

Round 22: [1dc in next 2 sts, inv dec] 6 times. (*18 sts*)

Round 23: [1dc in next st, inv dec] 6 times. (*12 sts*) Fasten off, leaving a long tail for sewing.

EARS

(make 2)

Using Champagne White, make a magic ring.

Round 1: 6dc into ring. (*6 sts*) PM at start of round.

Round 2: [1dc in next st, inv inc in next st] 3 times. (*9 sts*)

Round 3: [1dc in next 2 sts, inv inc in next st] 3 times. (*12 sts*)

Round 4: 1dc in each st.

Round 5: [1dc in next 2 sts, inv inc in next st] 4 times. (*16 sts*) Weave in end from magic ring.

Round 6: 1dc in each st.

Round 7: [1dc in next 3 sts, inv inc in next st] 4 times. (*20 sts*)

Rounds 8–18: 1dc in each st. Fasten off, leaving a long tail for sewing.

DUNGAREE STRAPS

(make 2)

Using Denim Blue, ch10. Fasten off, leaving a long tail for sewing.

MAKING UP AND FINISHING

Fold open sections of ears in half to create shaping. Position ears onto head and use yarn tails to sew into place (see page 124). Stuff head firmly. Lightly stuff arms. Place dungaree straps over upper portion of body to correspond with upper section of Denim Blue. Sew into place using yarn tails. Stuff body firmly.

Pin arms along neckline, ensuring that arms are positioned underneath dungaree straps. Sew head into place on top of body securing arms into seam as it is worked. Before finishing seam, add in additional stuffing to prevent neck section becoming floppy. Fasten off and bury all tails.

TOADSTOOL

Nothing says enchanted woodland quite like a red-capped toadstool. Why not crochet a few and make a fairy ring?

SKILL RATING ● ● ●

YARN AND MATERIALS

Cotton DK yarn (100% cotton)
 Red
 Taupe
 White
Pair of 5–6mm (⅜–¼in) safety eyes
Perlé Cotton No.8 in Black and White
Toy stuffing
Mylar® or piece of fairly stiff plastic (optional)
Plastic filling pellets (optional)

HOOK AND EQUIPMENT

3.25mm (US size D/3) crochet hook
Locking or ring stitch marker
Yarn needle

FINISHED MEASUREMENTS

7 x 10cm (2¾ x 4in) tall

ABBREVIATIONS

See page 126

TOADSTOOL CAP

Using Red, make a magic ring.
Round 1: 6dc into ring. (*6 sts*)
PM at start of round.
Round 2: [Inv inc in next st] 6 times. (*12 sts*)
Round 3: 1dc in each st.
Round 4: [1dc in next st, inv inc in next st] 6 times. (*18 sts*)
Round 5: [1dc in next 2 sts, inv inc in next st] 6 times. (*24 sts*)
Weave in end from magic ring (see page 124).
Round 6: [1dc in next 3 sts, inv inc in next st] 6 times. (*30 sts*)

Round 7: 1dc in each st.
Round 8: [1dc in next 4 sts, inv inc in next st] 6 times. (*36 sts*)
Round 9: [1dc in next 5 sts, inv inc in next st] 6 times. (*42 sts*)
Round 10: [1dc in next 6 sts, inv inc in next st] 6 times. (*48 sts*)
Round 11: 1dc in each st.
Round 12: [1dc in next 7 sts, inv inc in next st] 6 times. (*54 sts*)
Rounds 13–15: 1dc in each st.
Round 16: [1dc in next 7 sts, inv dec] 6 times. (*48 sts*)
Round 17: [1dc in next 6 sts, inv dec] 6 times. (*42 sts*)
Fasten off, leaving a long tail for sewing.
Position safety eyes at centre front, evenly spaced, and fasten securely (see page 124).
Sew face details using Perlé cotton and yarn needle, using Black for V-shaped mouth and White for cheeks (see page 125). Fasten off and secure all thread ends.

STALK

Using Taupe, make a magic ring.
Round 1: 6dc into ring, drawing up to make circle of sts. (*6 sts*)
PM at start of round.
Round 2: [Inv inc in next st] 6 times. (*12 sts*)
Round 3: [1dc in next st, inv inc in next st] 6 times. (*18 sts*)
Round 4: [1dc in next 2 sts, inv inc in next st] 6 times. (*24 sts*)
Round 5: [1dc in next 3 sts, inv inc in next st] 6 times. (*30 sts*)
Weave in end from magic ring.

Round 6: 1dcBLO in each st.
Round 7: [1dc in next 4 sts, inv inc in next st] 6 times. (*36 sts*)
Round 8: 1dc in each st.
(Optional: Cut a circle of Mylar® or fairly stiff plastic to correspond to base section and insert before cont.)
Round 9: [1dc in next 4 sts, inv dec] 6 times. (*30 sts*)
Round 10: [1dc in next 3 sts, inv dec] 6 times. (*24 sts*)
Round 11: [1dc in next 2 sts, inv dec] 6 times. (*18 sts*)
Rounds 12–15: 1dc in each st.
Round 16: [1dcFLO in next 2 sts, inv inc in next st] 6 times. (*24 sts*)
Round 17: [1dc in next 3 sts, inv inc in next st] 6 times. (*30 sts*)
Round 18: [1dc in next 4 sts, inv inc in next st] 6 times. (*36 sts*)
Round 19: [1dc in next 5 sts, inv inc in next st] 6 times. (*42 sts*)
Round 20: 1dc in each st, sl st in first st to join.
Fasten off, leaving a long tail for sewing.

SMALL ACCENT DOTS

(make 3)
Using White, make a magic ring.
Round 1: 6dc into ring, sl st in first st to join. (*6 sts*)
Fasten off, leaving a long tail for sewing.

LARGE ACCENT DOTS

(make 3)
Using White, make a magic ring.
Round 1: 6dc into ring. (*6 sts*)
PM at start of round.
Round 2: [Inv inc in next st] 6 times, sl st in first st to join. (*12 sts*)
Fasten off, leaving a long tail for sewing.

MAKING UP AND FINISHING

Position white accent dots around cap of toadstool and use tails to secure in place (see page 124). Stuff cap.
(Optional: Insert small bag of plastic pellets into stalk to add weight to base and fill remaining section with stuffing. Cut circle of Mylar® or fairly stiff plastic to correspond with top of stalk and place on top of stuffing.)
If you're not using plastic pellets or Mylar® or fairly stiff plastic, stuff the stalk.
Place cap onto stalk and use yarn tail to sew cap into position. Before finishing seam add in additional stuffing to prevent upper section becoming floppy.
Fasten off and bury all tails.

FOX

This friendly fox is ready for autumn with his smart green scarf. His smiley face is made with white accents that give him his unmistakable features.

SKILL RATING ● ● ●

YARN AND MATERIALS

Cotton DK yarn (100% cotton)
- Rust
- White
- Black
- Green

Pair of ⅜–¼in (5–6mm) safety eyes

Perlé Cotton No.8 in Black and Pink

Toy stuffing

HOOK AND EQUIPMENT

3.25mm (US size D/3) crochet hook

Locking or ring stitch marker

Yarn needle

Pins

FINISHED MEASUREMENTS

9.5 x 16cm (3¾ x 6¼in)

ABBREVIATIONS

See page 126

HEAD

Using Rust, make a magic ring.

Round 1: 6dc into ring. (*6 sts*)
PM at start of round.

Round 2: [Inv inc in next st] 6 times. (*12 sts*)

Round 3: [1dc in next st, inv inc in next st] 6 times. (*18 sts*)

Round 4: [1dc in next 2 sts, inv inc in next st] 6 times. (*24 sts*)

Round 5: [1dc in next 3 sts, inv inc in next st] 6 times. (*30 sts*)
Weave in end from magic ring (see page 124).

Round 6: [1dc in next 4 sts, inv inc in next st] 6 times. (*36 sts*)

Round 7: [1dc in next 5 sts, inv inc in next st] 6 times. (*42 sts*)

Round 8: [1dc in next 6 sts, inv inc in next st] 6 times. (*48 sts*)

Rounds 9–13: 1dc in each st.
Join in White.

Round 14: 18dc in White, 12dc in Rust, 18dc in White. (*48 sts*)

Round 15: 20dc in White, 8dc in Rust, 20dc in White.

Round 16: 22dc in White, 4dc in Rust, 22dc in White.

Round 17: 23dc in White, 2dc in Rust, 23dc in White.
Fasten off Rust and cont in White only.

Round 18: [1dc in next 6 sts, inv dec] 6 times. (*42 sts*)

Round 19: [1dc in next 5 sts, inv dec] 6 times. (*36 sts*)

Round 20: [1dc in next 4 sts, inv dec] 6 times. (*30 sts*)

Round 21: [1dc in next 3 sts, inv dec] 6 times. (*24 sts*)
Position safety eyes, evenly spaced at centre front of face, following yarn colours as a guide, and fasten securely (see page 124).
Sew face details using Perlé cotton and yarn needle, using Black for nose and V-shaped mouth and Pink for cheeks (see page 125).
Fasten off and secure all thread ends.

Round 22: [1dc in next 2 sts, inv dec] 6 times. (*18 sts*)

Round 23: [1dc in next st, inv dec] 6 times. (*12 sts*)
Fasten off, leaving a long tail for sewing.

ARMS

(make 2)

Using Black, make a magic ring.

Round 1: 6dc into ring. (*6 sts*)
PM at start of round.

Round 2: [Inv inc in next st] 6 times. (*12 sts*)

Round 3: 1dc in each st.

Round 4: 1dc in next 10 sts, inv dec. (*11 sts*)

Round 5: 1dc in next 9 sts, inv dec. (*10 sts*)
Fasten off Black and change to Rust.

Rounds 6–17: 1dc in each st.
Fasten off, leaving a long tail for sewing.

BODY

Worked from legs upwards.

FIRST LEG

Using Black, make a magic ring.

Round 1: 6dc into ring. (*6 sts*)
PM at start of round.

Round 2: [Inv inc in next st] 6 times. (*12 sts*)

Round 3: [1dc in next st, inv inc in next st] 6 times. (*18 sts*)

Rounds 4 and 5: 1dc in each st.
Fasten off Black and change to Rust.

Rounds 6–8: 1dc in each st.
Fasten off first leg, set aside.

SECOND LEG

Using Black, make a magic ring.

Round 1: 6dc into ring. (*6 sts*)
PM at start of round.

Round 2: [Inv inc in next st] 6 times. (*12 sts*)

Round 3: [1dc in next st, inv inc in next st] 6 times. (*18 sts*)

Rounds 4 and 5: 1dc in each st.
Fasten off Black and change to Rust.

Rounds 6–8: 1dc in each st.

Round 9: Place first leg next to second leg, work 18dc across first leg, then cont with 1dc in each st around second leg. (*36 sts*)

BODY

Rounds 10–16: 1dc in each st.

Round 17: [1dc in next 4 sts, inv dec] 6 times. (*30 sts*)

Rounds 18 and 19: 1dc in each st.

Round 20: [1dc in next 3 sts, inv dec] 6 times. (*24 sts*)

Round 21: 1dc in each st.

Round 22: [1dc in next 2 sts, inv dec] 6 times. (*18 sts*)

Round 23: [1dc in next st, inv dec] 6 times. (*12 sts*)
Fasten off, leaving a long tail for sewing.

TAIL

Using White, make a magic ring.

Round 1: 6dc into ring. (*6 sts*)
PM at start of round.

Round 2: [1dc in next st, inv inc in next st] 3 times. (*9 sts*)

Round 3: 1dc in each st.

Round 4: [1dc in next 2 sts, inv inc in next st] 3 times. (*12 sts*)

Round 5: 1dc in each st.
Fasten off White and change to Rust.

Round 6: [1dc in next 2 sts, inv inc in next st] 4 times. (*16 sts*)

Round 7: 1dc in each st.

Round 8: [1dc in next 2 sts, inv dec] 4 times. (*12 sts*)

Rounds 9–12: 1dc in each st.

Round 13: [1dc in next 2 sts, inv dec] 3 times. (*9 sts*)

Rounds 14–17: 1dc in each st.

Round 18: [1dc in next st, inv dec] 3 times. (*6 sts*)
Fasten off, leaving a long tail for sewing.

EARS

(make 2)

Using White, make a magic ring.

Round 1: 5dc into ring. (*5 sts*)
PM at start of round.

Round 2: 1dc in next 4 sts, inv inc in next st. (*6 sts*)
Fasten off White and change to Rust.

Round 3: [1dc in next st, inv inc in next st] 3 times. (*9 sts*)

Round 4: [1dc in next 2 sts, inv inc in next st] 3 times. (*12 sts*)

Rounds 5 and 6: 1dc in each st.
Fasten off, leaving a long tail for sewing.

SCARF

Using Green, ch4.

Row 1: Beg in 2nd ch from hook, 1dc in each ch. (*3 sts*)

Rows 2–50: Ch1 (does not count as a st), 1dc in each st.
Fasten off.

Cut 18 lengths of Green, each 7.5cm (3in) long. Using three strands held together, tie three lark's head knots at each end of the scarf (see page 125).

MAKING UP AND FINISHING

Position ears onto head and use yarn tails to sew into place (see page 124).

Stuff head firmly. Lightly stuff arms and tail.

Position tail onto back of body and sew into position using yarn tail.

Stuff body firmly.

Pin arms along neckline. Sew head into place on top of body, securing arms into seam as it is worked.

Before finishing seam, add in additional stuffing to prevent neck section becoming floppy.

Fasten off and bury all tails.

Tie scarf around fox's neck to finish.

FLOWER

This cheerful bloom will brighten any day. The simple petals can be worked in any colour to create your own bright posy.

YARN AND MATERIALS

Cotton DK yarn (100% cotton)
  Yellow
  Green
  Purple

Pair of 5–6mm (⅜–¼in) safety eyes

Perlé Cotton No.8 in Black and Pink

Toy stuffing

25.5cm (10in) of floristry or craft wire (15 gauge/1.5mm) (optional)

HOOK AND EQUIPMENT

3.25mm (US size D/3) crochet hook

Locking or ring stitch marker

Yarn needle

FINISHED MEASUREMENTS

9 x 12.5cm (3½ x 5in)

ABBREVIATIONS

See page 126

FLOWER CENTRE

Using Yellow, make a magic ring.

Round 1: 6dc into ring. (*6 sts*)
PM at start of round.

Round 2: [Inv inc in next st] 6 times. (*12 sts*)

Round 3: [1dc in next st, inv inc in next st] 6 times. (*18 sts*)

Round 4: [1dc in next 2 sts, inv inc in next st] 6 times. (*24 sts*)

Round 5: [1dc in next 3 sts, inv inc in next st] 6 times. (*30 sts*)
Weave in end from magic ring (see page 124).

Round 6: 1dcBLO in each st.

Rounds 7 and 8: 1dc in each st.
Position safety eyes at front of flower centre, evenly spaced, and fasten securely (see page 124). Sew face details using Perlé cotton and yarn needle, using Black for V-shaped mouth and Pink for cheeks (see page 125). Fasten off and secure all thread ends.

Round 9: [1dc in next 3 sts, inv dec] 6 times. (*24 sts*)

Beg filling with small pieces of toy stuffing, cont adding as dec rounds are worked.

Round 10: [Inv dec] 6 times. (*12 sts*)

Round 11: [Inv dec] 6 times. (*6 sts*)
Add final toy stuffing as needed. Fasten off.
Cut yarn, thread tail into a yarn needle and close opening by weaving through back loops only. Fasten off and bury tail through body of flower centre.

STEM

Using Green, make a magic ring.

Round 1: 5dc into ring. (*5 sts*)
PM at start of round.

Rounds 2–22: 1dc in each st.

Round 23: [Inv inc in next st] 5 times. (*10 sts*)

Round 24: 1dc in each st.

Round 25: [1dc in next st, inv inc in next st] 5 times. (*15 sts*)
Fasten off, leaving a long tail for sewing.
(Optional: Fold floristry wire in half and insert into stem.)

PETALS

(make 6)

Using Purple, make a magic ring.

Round 1: 6dc into ring. (*6 sts*)

PM at start of round.

Round 2: [Inv inc in next st] 6 times. (*12 sts*)

Round 3: [1dc in next 3 sts, 1htr in next 3 sts] twice.

Round 4: [1dc in next 2 sts, inv inc in next st] 4 times. (*16 sts*)

Rounds 5 and 6: 1dc in each st. Weave in end from magic ring.

Round 7: [1dc in next 2 sts, inv dec] 4 times. (*12 sts*)

Round 8: [1dc in next 4 sts, inv dec] twice. (*10 sts*)

Fasten off, leaving a long tail for sewing.

MAKING UP AND FINISHING

Place petals, folded flat, around outer part of flower centre. Use yarn tails to sew in place into unworked front loops (see page 124).

Place wide portion of stem onto back of flower centre and sew in place using yarn tail, ensuring that all wire ends, if using, are concealed. Fasten off and bury all tails.

SNAIL

This charming character has a colourful coiled shell on his back; team your two favourite shades to make your own fun snail.

SKILL RATING ● ● ○

YARN AND MATERIALS

Cotton DK yarn (100% cotton)
  Light Orange
  Dark Orange
  Caramel
Toy stuffing
Pair of 5–6mm (⅜–¼in) safety eyes
Perlé Cotton No.8 in Black and White
Floristry or craft wire (15 gauge/1.5mm) (optional)

HOOK AND EQUIPMENT

3.25mm (US size D/3) crochet hook
Locking or ring stitch marker
Yarn needle

FINISHED MEASUREMENTS

10 x 8cm (4 x 3¼in)

ABBREVIATIONS

See page 126

SNAIL SHELL

Using Light Orange, make a magic ring.
Round 1: 6dc into ring. (*6 sts*)
PM at start of round.
Round 2: 1dc in each st.
Round 3: [Inv inc in next st] 6 times. (*12 sts*)
Round 4: 1dc in each st.
Rounds 5–8: Change to Dark Orange, 1dc in each st.
Rounds 9–12: Change to Light Orange, 1dc in each st.
Beg lightly stuffing with small pieces of toy stuffing, cont adding as shell is worked but take care that finished shell is not too firmly stuffed to roll up.
Rounds 13–16: Change to Dark Orange, 1dc in each st.
Rounds 17–20: Change to Light Orange, 1dc in each st.
Rounds 21–24: Change to Dark Orange, 1dc in each st.
Rounds 25–28: Change to Light Orange, 1dc in each st.
Round 29: Change to Dark Orange [1dc in next st, inv inc in next st] 6 times. (*18 sts*)
Rounds 30–32: 1dc in each st.
Rounds 33–36: Change to Light Orange, 1dc in each st.
Rounds 37–40: Change to Dark Orange, 1dc in each st.
Rounds 41–44: Change to Light Orange, 1dc in each st.
Rounds 45–48: Change to Dark Orange, 1dc in each st.

At end of Round 48, sl st in first st to join.
Fasten off, leaving a long tail for sewing.

ANTENNAE

(make 2)
Using Caramel, make a magic ring.
Round 1: 4dc into ring, sl st in first st to join. (*4 sts*)
Ch4.
Fasten off, leaving a long tail for sewing.

HEAD AND BODY

Using Caramel, make a magic ring.
Round 1: 6dc into ring. (*6 sts*)
PM at start of round.
Round 2: [Inv inc in next st] 6 times. (*12 sts*)
Round 3: [1dc in next st, inv inc in next st] 6 times. (*18 sts*)
Round 4: [1dc in next 2 sts, inv inc in next st] 6 times. (*24 sts*)
Round 5: [1dc in next 3 sts, inv inc in next st] 6 times. (*30 sts*)
Weave in end from magic ring (see page 124).
Rounds 6–10: 1dc in each st.
Place antennae on top of head and sew into place with yarn tails (see page 124).
Position safety eyes at centre front of the head, evenly spaced, and fasten securely (see page 124). Sew face details using Perlé cotton and yarn needle, using Black for V-shaped mouth and Pink for cheeks (see page 125). Fasten off and secure all thread ends.

Round 11: [1dc in next 3 sts, inv dec] 6 times. (*24 sts*)

Beg filling with small pieces of toy stuffing, cont adding as body is worked.

Round 12: [1dc in next 2 sts, inv dec] 6 times. (*18 sts*)

Rounds 13–31: 1dc in each st.

Round 32: [1dc in next st, inv dec] 6 times. (*12 sts*)

Rounds 33–35: 1dc in each st. (Optional: Fold wire in half and insert into body from head to tail.)

Round 36: [Inv dec] 6 times. (*6 sts*)

Round 37: 1dc in each st.

Add final toy stuffing as needed. Fasten off.

Cut yarn, thread tail into a yarn needle and close opening by weaving through front loops only. Fasten off and bury tail through body of snail.

MAKING UP AND FINISHING

Fold the snail body to make L shape – if using wire this will hold its position, if not using wire use yarn tail to work a couple of stitches at bend to hold in place. Begin rolling shell section, working from narrow end inwards, using yarn tail to secure shell in shape. Place rolled shell onto back of snail and use yarn tail to sew into place. Fasten off and bury all tails.

FROG

Bright green and with long legs ready to bounce – this happy frog with his googly eyes is simple and fun to make.

SKILL RATING ● ● ●

YARN AND MATERIALS
Cotton DK yarn (100% cotton)
Green
White
Pair of 5–6mm (⅜–¼in) safety eyes
Perlé Cotton No.8 in Black and Pink
Toy stuffing

HOOK AND EQUIPMENT
3.25mm (US size D/3) crochet hook
Locking or ring stitch marker
Yarn needle

FINISHED MEASUREMENTS
8 x 8cm (3¼ x 3¼in)

ABBREVIATIONS
See page 126

EYES

(make 2)
Using Green, make a magic ring.
Round 1: 6dc into ring. (*6 sts*)
PM at start of round.
Round 2: [Inv inc in next st] 6 times. (*12 sts*)
Rounds 3–5: 1dc in each st.
Fasten off, leaving a long tail for sewing.

EYE ACCENTS

(make 2)
Using White, make a magic ring.
Round 1: 6dc into ring, sl st in first st to join. (*6 sts*)
Fasten off, leaving a long tail for sewing.
Position safety eye at centre front of each eye accent and fasten securely (see page 124).

HEAD AND BODY

Using Green, make a magic ring.
Round 1: 6dc into ring. (*6 sts*)
PM at start of round.
Round 2: [Inv inc in next st] 6 times. (*12 sts*)
Round 3: [1dc in next st, inv inc in next st] 6 times. (*18 sts*)
Round 4: [1dc in next 2 sts, inv inc in next st] 6 times. (*24 sts*)
Round 5: [1dc in next 3 sts, inv inc in next st] 6 times. (*30 sts*)
Weave in end from magic ring (see page 124).
Round 6: [1dc in next 4 sts, inv inc in next st] 6 times. (*36 sts*)

Rounds 7 and 8: 1dc in each st.
Round 9: [1dc in next 5 sts, inv inc in next st] 6 times. (*42 sts*)
Rounds 10–17: 1dc in each st.
Sew face details using Perlé cotton and yarn needle, using Black for V-shaped mouth and Pink for cheeks (see page 125). Fasten off and secure all thread ends.
Round 18: [1dc in next 6 sts, inv inc in next st] 6 times. (*48 sts*)
Round 19: 1dc in each st.
Beg filling with small pieces of toy stuffing, cont adding as dec rounds are worked.
Round 20: [1dc in next 6 sts, inv dec] 6 times. (*42 sts*)
Round 21: [1dc in next 5 sts, inv dec] 6 times. (*36 sts*)
Round 22: [1dc in next 4 sts, inv dec] 6 times. (*30 sts*)
Round 23: [1dc in next 3 sts, inv dec] 6 times. (*24 sts*)
Round 24: [1dc in next 2 sts, inv dec] 6 times. (*18 sts*)
Round 25: [1dc in next st, inv dec] 6 times. (*12 sts*)
Add final toy stuffing as needed.
Round 26: [Inv dec] 6 times. (*6 sts*)
Fasten off.
Cut yarn, thread tail into a yarn needle and close opening by weaving through front loops only. Fasten off and bury tail through body of frog.

LEGS

(make 2)

Using Green, make a magic ring.

Round 1: 6dc into ring. (*6 sts*)

PM at start of round.

Rounds 2–24: 1dc in each st.

TOES

Round 25: [1sl stFLO in next st, ch6, beg in 2nd ch from hook, sl st in next 5 ch] 3 times, sl st in last st to join.

Fasten off, leaving a long tail for sewing.

MAKING UP AND FINISHING

Place eye accent on front of each main eye and sew in place (see page 125). Place eyes onto top of head and use yarn tails to sew into place. Add small amount of stuffing before completing seam.

Working on each leg in turn, fold in half to align end of leg and foot, with toes outermost. Use yarn tail to add a couple of stitches to secure bend. Place leg onto side of body and sew into place using yarn tail. Repeat for second leg. Fasten off and bury all tails.

BUTTERFLY

A bold butterfly with pretty accents on her wings – and because these only use a small amount of yarn they are ideal for using up your favourite shades from your stash.

SKILL RATING ● ● ●

YARN AND MATERIALS

Cotton DK yarn (100% cotton)
  Orange
  Pink
  Green
  Purple
  Yellow
Pair of 5–6mm (⅜–¼in) safety eyes
Perlé Cotton No.8 in Black and Pink
Toy stuffing

HOOK AND EQUIPMENT

3.25mm (US size D/3) crochet hook
Locking or ring stitch marker
Yarn needle

FINISHED MEASUREMENTS

11.5 x 12.5cm (4½ x 5in)

ABBREVIATIONS

See page 126

BUTTERFLY ANTENNAE

(make 2)
Using Orange, make a magic ring.
Round 1: 4dc into ring, sl st in first st to join. (*4 sts*)
Ch4.
Fasten off, leaving a long tail for sewing.

HEAD AND BODY

Using Orange, make a magic ring.
Round 1: 6dc into ring. (*6 sts*)
PM at start of round.
Round 2: [Inv inc in next st] 6 times. (*12 sts*)
Round 3: [1dc in next st, inv inc in next st] 6 times. (*18 sts*)
Round 4: [1dc in next 2 sts, inv inc in next st] 6 times. (*24 sts*)
Round 5: [1dc in next 3 sts, inv inc in next st] 6 times. (*30 sts*)
Weave in end from magic ring (see page 124).
Round 6: [1dc in next 4 sts, inv inc in next st] 6 times. (*36 sts*)
Rounds 7–13: 1dc in each st.
Place antennae on top of head and sew into place using yarn tails (see page 125).
Position safety eyes at centre front of head, evenly spaced, and fasten securely (see page 124).

Sew face details using Perlé cotton and yarn needle, using Black for V-shaped mouth and Pink for cheeks (see page 125). Fasten off and secure all thread ends.
Round 14: [1dc in next 4 sts, inv dec] 6 times. (*30 sts*)
Round 15: [1dc in next 3 sts, inv dec] 6 times. (*24 sts*)
Beg filling with small pieces of toy stuffing, cont adding as body is worked.
Round 16: [1dc in next 2 sts, inv dec] 6 times. (*18 sts*)
Round 17: [1dc in next st, inv dec] 6 times. (*12 sts*)
Round 18: [1dc in next st, inv inc in next st] 6 times. (*18 sts*)
Round 19: [1dc in next 2 sts, inv inc in next st] 6 times. (*24 sts*)
Rounds 20–24: 1dc in each st.
Round 25: [1dc in next 2 sts, inv dec] 6 times. (*18 sts*)
Round 26: [1dc in next st, inv dec] 6 times. (*12 sts*)
Round 27: [1dc in next st, inv inc in next st] 6 times. (*18 sts*)
Rounds 28–32: 1dc in each st.
Round 33: [1dc in next st, inv dec] 6 times. (*12 sts*)

Round 34: [1dc in next 2 sts, inv dec] 3 times. (*9 sts*)
Round 35: 1dc in each st.
Round 36: [1dc in next st, inv dec] 3 times. (*6 sts*)
Round 37: 1dc in each st.
Add final toy stuffing as needed.
Fasten off.
Cut yarn, thread tail into a yarn needle and close opening by weaving through front loops only.
Fasten off and bury tail through body.

LARGE WINGS
(make 2)
Using Pink, make a magic ring.
Round 1: 6dc into ring. (*6 sts*)
PM at start of round.
Round 2: [Inv inc in next st] 6 times. (*12 sts*)
Round 3: [1dc in next st, inv inc in next st] 6 times. (*18 sts*)
Round 4: [1dc in next 2 sts, inv inc in next st] 6 times. (*24 sts*)
Round 5: [1dc in next 3 sts, inv inc in next st] 6 times. (*30 sts*)
Weave in end from magic ring.
Rounds 6–8: 1dc in each st.

Round 9: [1dc in next 13 sts, inv dec] twice. (*28 sts*)
Round 10: [1dc in next 12 sts, inv dec] twice. (*26 sts*)
Round 11: [1dc in next 11 sts, inv dec] twice. (*24 sts*)
Round 12: [1dc in next 10 sts, inv dec] twice. (*22 sts*)
Round 13: [1dc in next 9 sts, inv dec] twice. (*20 sts*)
Round 14: [1dc in next 8 sts, inv dec] twice, sl st in first st to join. (*18 sts*)
Fasten off, leaving a long tail for sewing.

LARGE WING ACCENTS

(make 2)

Using Green, make a magic ring.

Round 1: 6dc into ring. (*6 sts*)
PM at start of round.

Round 2: [Inv inc in next st] 6 times. (*12 sts*)

Round 3: [1dc in next st, inv inc in next st] 6 times, sl st in first st to join. (*18 sts*)
Fasten off, leaving a long tail for sewing.

SMALL WINGS

(make 2)

Using Purple, make a magic ring.

Round 1: 6dc into ring. (*6 sts*)
PM at start of round.

Round 2: [Inv inc in next st] 6 times. (*12 sts*)

Round 3: [1dc in next st, inv inc in next st] 6 times. (*18 sts*)
Weave in end from magic ring.

Rounds 4–6: 1dc in each st.

Round 7: [1dc in next 7 sts, inv dec] twice. (*16 sts*)

Round 8: [1dc in next 6 sts, inv dec] twice. (*14 sts*)

Round 9: [1dc in next 5 sts, inv dec] twice. (*12 sts*)

Round 10: [1dc in next 4 sts, inv dec] twice, sl st in first st to join. (*10 sts*)
Fasten off, leaving a long tail for sewing.

SMALL WING ACCENTS

(make 2)

Using Yellow, make a magic ring.

Round 1: 6dc into ring. (*6 sts*)
PM at start of round.

Round 2: [Inv inc in next st] 6 times, sl st in first st to join. (*12 sts*)
Fasten off, leaving a long tail for sewing.

MAKING UP AND FINISHING

Place large wing accent onto each large wing and sew in place using yarn tails, being sure to work through top layer of wing only so that stitches aren't visible from back.

Repeat to sew small wing accents onto each small wing.

Place large wing on side of body along upper portion, sew into place using yarn tail. Repeat to secure second large wing on other side.

Position small wing onto side of body below large wing and sew into place using yarn tail. Repeat to secure second small wing on other side.

Fasten off and bury all tails.

CHAPTER 4

DAILY LIFE

CRAYONS

A trio of colourful classroom classics that are quick and easy to make – you can crochet more in a whole rainbow of colours, too.

SKILL RATING ● ● ○ ○

YARN AND MATERIALS

Cotton DK yarn (100% cotton)
  Dark Pink
  Dark Turquoise
  Dark Yellow
  Light Pink
  Light Turquoise
  Light Yellow
  Black
Mylar® or piece of fairly stiff plastic (optional)
Toy stuffing
Pair of 5–6mm (⅜–¼in) safety eyes
Perlé Cotton No.8 in Black and Pink

HOOK AND EQUIPMENT

3.25mm (US size D/3) crochet hook
Locking or ring stitch marker
Yarn needle

FINISHED MEASUREMENTS

4 x 12.5cm (1½ x 5in)

ABBREVIATIONS

See page 126

CRAYONS

(make 1 in each colourway)
Using Dark Pink (Dark Turquoise/Dark Yellow), make a magic ring.
Round 1: 6dc into ring. (*6 sts*)
PM at start of round.
Round 2: [Inv inc in next st] 6 times. (*12 sts*)
Round 3: [1dc in next st, inv inc in next st] 6 times. (*18 sts*)
Round 4: [1dc in next 2 sts, inv inc in next st] 6 times. (*24 sts*)
Round 5: 1dcBLO in each st.
Weave in end from magic ring (see page 124).
(Optional: Cut two circles of Mylar® or fairly stiff plastic to correspond to base section and insert one before cont. Set aside second circle.)
Rounds 6–8: 1dc in each st.
Fasten off Dark Pink (Dark Turquoise/Dark Yellow), join in Light Pink (Light Turquoise/Light Yellow).
Rounds 9 and 10: 1dc in each st.
Join in Black.
Round 11: Using Black, 1dc in each st.
Fasten off Black.
Beg filling with small pieces of toy stuffing, cont adding as body is worked.
Rounds 12–23: Using Light Pink (Light Turquoise/Light Yellow), 1dc in each st.
Position safety eyes at centre front of the crayon, evenly spaced, and fasten securely (see page 124).

Sew face details using Perlé cotton and yarn needle, using Black for V-shaped mouth and Pink for cheeks (see page 125). Fasten off and secure all thread ends.
Join in Black.
Round 24: Using Black, 1dc in each st.
Fasten off Black.
Rounds 25 and 26: Using Light Pink (Light Turquoise/Light Yellow), 1dc in each st.
Fasten off Light Pink (Light Turquoise/Light Yellow), join in Dark Pink (Dark Turquoise/Dark Yellow).
Rounds 27 and 28: 1dc in each st.
Round 29: 1dcBLO in each st.
Round 30: [1dc in next 2 sts, inv dec] 6 times. (*18 sts*)
Finishing stuffing centre section.
(Optional: Add in second Mylar® circle.)
Round 31: 1dc in each st.
Beg stuffing upper section.
Round 32: [1dc in next st, inv dec] 6 times. (*12 sts*)
Rounds 33 and 34: 1dc in each st.
Add final toy stuffing as needed.
Round 35: [Inv dec] 6 times. (*6 sts*)
Round 36: 1dc in each st.
Fasten off.
Cut yarn, thread tail into a yarn needle and close opening by weaving through front loops only.

MAKING UP AND FINISHING

Bury all tails.

PAINTBRUSH

Add a flash of colour to your life with this classic paintbrush, complete with its own bright paint splatter!

SKILL RATING ● ● ○

YARN AND MATERIALS

Cotton DK yarn (100% cotton)
- Light Brown
- Turquoise
- Light Grey
- Pink
- Mid Beige

Toy stuffing

12in (30cm) of floristry or craft wire (15 gauge/1.5mm) (optional)

Pair of 5–6mm (⅜–¼in) safety eyes

Perlé Cotton No.8 in Black and White

HOOK AND EQUIPMENT

3.25mm (US size D/3) crochet hook

Locking or ring stitch marker

Yarn needle

FINISHED MEASUREMENTS

Paintbrush: 3 x 15cm (1¼ x 6in)

Paint splatter: 5 x 6.5cm (2 x 2½in)

ABBREVIATIONS

See page 126

PAINTBRUSH HANDLE

Using Light Brown, make a magic ring.

Round 1: 6dc into ring. (*6 sts*)
PM at start of round.

Rounds 2–6: 1dc in each st.
Weave in end from magic ring (see page 124).
Join in Turquoise.

Rounds 7 and 8: Using Turquoise, 1dc in each st.
Fasten off Turquoise.

Rounds 9–13: Using Light Brown, 1dc in each st.

Round 14: [1dc in next 2 sts, inv inc in next st] twice. (*8 sts*)

Rounds 15–24: 1dc in each st.
Fasten off Light Brown, join in Light Grey.

Rounds 25–27: 1dc in each st.

Round 28: [1dc in next st, inv inc in next st] 4 times. (*12 sts*)
Lightly stuff.
(Optional: Insert floristry wire, allowing enough to fill bristles later.)
Fasten off, leaving a long tail for sewing.

PAINTBRUSH BRISTLES

Using Pink, make a magic ring.

Round 1: 4dc into ring. (*4 sts*)
PM at start of round.

Round 2: [1dc in next st, inv inc in next st] twice. (*6 sts*)

Round 3: [1dc in next 2 sts, inv inc in next st] twice. (*8 sts*)

Round 4: [1dc in next st, inv inc in next st] 4 times. (*12 sts*)

Round 5: [1dc in next st, inv inc in next st] 6 times. (*18 sts*)
Weave in end from magic ring.

Round 6: 1dc in each st.

Round 7: [1dc in next 2 sts, inv inc in next st] 6 times. (*24 sts*)
Join in Mid Beige.

Round 8: [3dc in Pink, 1dc in Mid Beige] 6 times.

Round 9: [2dc in Pink, 2dc in Mid Beige] 6 times.

Round 10: [1dc in Pink, 3dc in Mid Beige] 6 times.
Fasten off Pink.

Round 11: 1dc in each st.
Position safety eyes at centre front of bristles, evenly spaced, and fasten securely (see page 124).

Sew face details using Perlé cotton and yarn needle, using Black for V-shaped mouth and White for cheeks (see page 125). Fasten off and secure all thread ends.

Beg stuffing with small pieces of toy stuffing, cont adding as dec rounds are worked.

Round 12: [1dc in next st, inv dec] 8 times. (*16 sts*)

Round 13: [1dc in next 2 sts, inv dec] 4 times. (*12 sts*)

Add final toy stuffing as needed.

Round 14: [Inv dec] 6 times. (*6 sts*)

Fasten off and cut yarn, leaving a long tail for sewing, thread tail into a yarn needle and close opening by weaving through front loops only.

PAINT SPLATTER

Using Pink, make a magic ring.

Round 1: 6dc into ring. (*6 sts*)

PM at start of round.

Round 2: [Inv inc in next st] 6 times. (*12 sts*)

Round 3: [1dc in next st, inv inc in next st] 6 times. (*18 sts*)

Round 4: [1dc in next 2 sts, inv inc in next st] 6 times. (*24 sts*)

Round 5: [1dc in next 3 sts, inv inc in next st] 6 times. (*30 sts*)

Round 6: 4tr in next st, skip next st, sl st in next 3 sts, (2tr, 2dtr, 2tr) in next st, skip next st, sl st in next 5 sts, ch4, 4htr in 2nd ch from hook, sl st in next 2 ch, sl st in next 5 sts, (2tr, 2dtr, 2tr) in next st, skip next st, sl st in next 3 sts, 4tr in next st, skip next st, sl st in next 2 sts, ch3, 4htr in 2nd ch from hook, sl st in next ch, skip next st, sl st in last 3 sts. Fasten off.

MAKING UP AND FINISHING

Weave in ends on paint splatter. Position paintbrush bristles onto paintbrush handle and use yarn tails to sew into place, ensuring any wire, if used, is concealed. Sew the paint splatter under the bristles if desired. Fasten off and bury all tails.

PLANT

Brighten your home with this happy houseplant –
she's the ultimate in low-maintenance greenery!

SKILL RATING ● ● ●

YARN AND MATERIALS
Cotton DK yarn (100% cotton)
  Light Green
  Bright Green
  Mid Green
  Dark Green
  Brown
  Yellow
  Beige

Mylar® or piece of fairly stiff plastic
(optional)
Pair of 5–6mm (⅜–¼in) safety eyes
Perlé Cotton No.8 in Black and Pink
Plastic filling pellets (optional)
Toy stuffing

HOOK AND EQUIPMENT
3.25mm (US size D/3) crochet hook
Locking or ring stitch marker
Yarn needle

FINISHED MEASUREMENTS
7.5 x 9.5cm (3 x 3¾in) wide

ABBREVIATIONS
See page 126

PLANT LEAVES
(make 6, in range of greens)
Using Green, ch24 leaving a long tail at start.

FIRST SIDE
Sl st in 2nd ch from hook, [sl st in next ch, ch3, sl st in first ch from hook, 1dc in next 2 ch, sl st in next ch] twice, [sl st in next ch, ch4, sl st in first ch from hook, 1dc in next 3 ch, sl sl in next ch] twice, [sl st in next ch, ch5, sl st in first ch from hook, 1dc in next 4 ch, sl sl in next ch] twice, [sl st in next ch, ch6, sl st in first ch from hook, 1dc in next 5 ch, sl st in next ch] twice, [sl st in next ch, ch7, sl st in first ch from hook, 1dc in next 6 ch, sl st in next ch] twice, 1dc in next ch, 2dc in last ch, do not turn but cont down opp side of chain to work second side.

SECOND SIDE
1dc in next ch, [sl st in next ch, ch7, sl st in first ch from hook, 1dc in next 6 ch, sl st in next ch] twice, [sl st in next ch, ch6, sl st in first ch from hook, 1dc in next 5 ch, sl st in next ch] twice, [sl st in next ch, ch5, sl st in first ch from hook, 1dc in next 4 ch, sl st in next ch] twice, [sl st in next ch, ch4, sl st in first ch from hook, 1dc in next 3 ch, sl st in next ch] twice, [sl st in next ch, ch3, sl st in first ch from hook, 1dc in next 2 ch, sl st in next ch] twice. Fasten off, leaving a long tail for sewing. Weave tail down centre of leaf so that both tails are available to secure to soil later.

SOIL
Using Brown, make a magic ring.
Round 1: 6dc into ring. (*6 sts*)
PM at start of round.
Round 2: [Inv inc in next st] 6 times. (*12 sts*)
Round 3: [1dc in next st, inv inc in next st] 6 times. (*18 sts*)
Round 4: [1dc in next 2 sts, inv inc in next st] 6 times. (*24 sts*)
Round 5: [1dc in next 3 sts, inv inc in next st] 6 times. (*30 sts*)
Weave in end from magic ring (see page 124).
Round 6: [1dc in next 4 sts, inv inc in next st] 6 times. (*36 sts*)
Round 7: [1dc in next 5 sts, inv inc in next st] 6 times. (*42 sts*)
Round 8: [1dc in next 6 sts, inv inc in next st] 6 times. (*48 sts*)
Fasten off, leaving a long tail for sewing.

POT
Using Yellow, make a magic ring.
Round 1: 6dc into ring. (*6 sts*)
PM at start of round.
Round 2: [Inv inc in next st] 6 times. (*12 sts*)
Round 3: [1dc in next st, inv inc in next st] 6 times. (*18 sts*)
Round 4: [1dc in next 2 sts, inv inc in next st] 6 times. (*24 sts*)
Round 5: [1dc in next 3 sts, inv inc in next st] 6 times. (*30 sts*)
Weave in end from magic ring.
Round 6: [1dc in next 4 sts, inv inc in next st] 6 times. (*36 sts*)
Round 7: [1dc in next 5 sts, inv inc in next st] 6 times. (*42 sts*)
Round 8: 1dcBLO in each st.
(Optional: Cut a circle of Mylar® or fairly stiff plastic to correspond to base section and insert it before cont.)

Rounds 9–12: 1dc in each st.
Round 13: [1dc in next 6 sts, inv inc in next st] 6 times. (*48 sts*)
Rounds 14–17: 1dc in each st.
Fasten off Yellow, join in Beige.
Round 18: 1dc in each st.
Round 19: 1dcFLO in each st.
Round 20: 1dc in each st, sl st in first st to join.
Fasten off.
Position safety eyes at centre front of pot, evenly spaced, and fasten securely (see page 124). Sew face details using Perlé cotton and yarn needle, using Black for V-shaped mouth and Pink for cheeks (see page 125). Fasten off and secure all thread ends.

MAKING UP AND FINISHING
Use yarn tails to secure leaves into place on soil (see page 124). (Optional: Insert small bag of plastic filling pellets into base of pot.) Begin stuffing pot.
Fold down upper portion of pot slightly and using unworked back loops place soil in top of pot and begin sewing into place. Finish stuffing pot beneath soil before completing seam.
Fasten off and bury all tails.

BOOK

With his deep purple cover and golden stitches this classic book could be a Halloween book of spells, or your latest romance read.

SKILL RATING ●●○

YARN AND MATERIALS
Cotton DK yarn (100% cotton)
  Purple
  Parchment
  Gold
Plastic canvas (optional)
Pair of 5–6mm (⅜–¼in) safety eyes
Perlé Cotton No.8 in Black and Pink
Toy stuffing

HOOK AND EQUIPMENT
3.25mm (US size D/3) crochet hook
Locking or ring stitch marker
Yarn needle

FINISHED MEASUREMENTS
6.5 x 9 x 4cm (2½ x 3½ x 1½in)

ABBREVIATIONS
See page 126

BOOK COVER
Using Purple, ch39.
Row 1: Beg in 2nd ch from hook, 1dc in each ch to end. (*38 sts*)
Rows 2–21: Ch1 (does not count as a st), 1dc in each st.
Row 22: Work around entire rectangle with 1dc in each st and 2dc in each corner st, sl st in first st to join.
Fasten off, leaving an extra-long tail for sewing.

BOOK PAGES
Using Parchment, ch8.
Row 1: Beg in 2nd ch from hook, 1dc in each ch to end. (*7 sts*)
Rows 2–40: Ch1 (does not count as a st), 1dc in each st.
Fasten off, leaving a long tail for sewing.

MAKING UP AND FINISHING
Cut plastic canvas to fit inside cover, two pieces approx. 8 x 6cm (3¼ x 2¼in) and one approx. 8 x 3.5cm (3¼ x 1⅜in). Position onto WS of cover with single smaller piece as spine and larger two on either side as front and back. Sew in place with yarn tail, adding small amount of stuffing behind spine piece, to create light padding. Sew three lines in Gold evenly spaced down spine.
Position safety eyes at centre front of front cover, evenly spaced, and fasten securely, through both plastic canvas and crochet (see page 124).
Sew face details using Perlé cotton and yarn needle, using Black for V-shaped mouth and Pink for cheeks (see page 125). Fasten off and secure all thread ends.
With RS outermost, place one short end of book page strip along top of spine of book cover and sew into place. Fold front cover up towards book page strip and use yarn tail to sew book page strip into place around top, side and bottom of front cover. Sew other short end of book page strip securely to bottom of spine. Fold back cover over and sew book page strip into place to back cover in same way, stuffing as you work to fill inside book. Fasten off and bury all tails.

MUG

This mug of coffee is never empty – what could be better? He's worked in a variegated yarn for a unique finish to this crochet crockery.

YARN AND MATERIALS

Cotton DK yarn (100% cotton)
    Variegated Blue
    Light Brown
Mylar® or piece of fairly stiff plastic (optional)
Pair of 5–6mm (⅜–¼in) safety eyes
Perlé Cotton No.8 in Black and Pink
Toy stuffing
4in (10cm) of floristry or craft wire (15 gauge/1.5mm) (optional)

HOOK AND EQUIPMENT

3.25mm (US size D/3) crochet hook
Locking or ring stitch marker
Yarn needle

FINISHED MEASUREMENTS

9 x 6.5cm (3½ x 2½in) (incl handle)

ABBREVIATIONS

See page 126

MUG

Using Variegated Blue, make a magic ring.
Round 1: 6dc into ring. (*6 sts*) PM at start of round.
Round 2: [Inv inc in next st] 6 times. (*12 sts*)
Round 3: [1dc in next st, inv inc in next st] 6 times. (*18 sts*)
Round 4: [1dc in next 2 sts, inv inc in next st] 6 times. (*24 sts*)
Round 5: [1dc in next 3 sts, inv inc in next st] 6 times. (*30 sts*)
Weave in end from magic ring (see page 124).
Round 6: [1dc in next 4 sts, inv inc in next st] 6 times. (*36 sts*)
Round 7: [1dc in next 5 sts, inv inc in next st] 6 times. (*42 sts*)
Round 8: 1dcBLO in each st.

(Optional: Cut two circles of Mylar® or fairly stiff plastic to correspond to base section and insert one before cont. Set aside second circle.)
Rounds 9–23: 1dc in each st. Position safety eyes at centre front of mug, evenly spaced, and fasten securely (see page 124).
Sew face details using Perlé cotton and yarn needle, using Black for V-shaped mouth and Pink for cheeks (see page 125). Fasten off and secure all thread ends.
Round 24: 1dcFLO in each st.
Round 25: 1dc in each st, sl st in first st to join.
Fasten off.

MUG HANDLE

Using Variegated Blue, make a magic ring.

Round 1: 6dc into ring. (*6 sts*) PM at start of round.

Rounds 2–17: 1dc in each st. Stuff lightly.

(Optional: insert floristry wire.)

Fasten off and cut yarn, leaving a long tail for sewing, thread tail into a yarn needle and close opening by weaving through front loops only.

COFFEE TOP

Using Light Brown, make a magic ring.

Round 1: 6dc into ring. (*6 sts*) PM at start of round.

Round 2: [Inv inc in next st] 6 times. (*12 sts*)

Round 3: [1dc in next st, inv inc in next st] 6 times. (*18 sts*)

Round 4: [1dc in next 2 sts, inv inc in next st] 6 times. (*24 sts*)

Round 5: [1dc in next 3 sts, inv inc in next st] 6 times. (*30 sts*) Weave in end from magic ring.

Round 6: [1dc in next 4 sts, inv inc in next st] 6 times. (*36 sts*)

Round 7: [1dc in next 5 sts, inv inc in next st] 6 times, sl st in first st to join. (*42 sts*) Fasten off, leaving a long tail for sewing.

MAKING UP AND FINISHING

Place handle onto side of mug, ensuring that face detail is facing forward. Sew into place using yarn tail (see page 124).

Begin stuffing mug.

Fold down upper portion of mug slightly and using unworked back loops place coffee top in top of mug and begin sewing into place. Stop once coffee top is secure halfway around.

(Optional: Add second Mylar® circle.)

Fill mug with stuffing. Complete seam.

Fasten off and bury all tails.

TOOTHBRUSH AND TOOTHPASTE

A cool duo set that are a fun pair of characters to create.
The simple shapes are quick to make and instantly recognisable.

SKILL RATING ● ● ●

YARN AND MATERIALS

Cotton DK yarn (100% cotton)
  Denim Blue
  White
  Dark Turquoise
  Light Turquoise

Toy stuffing

2 or 3 lolly (popsicle) sticks (optional)

Pair of 5–6mm (⅜–¼in) safety eyes

Perlé Cotton No.8 in Black and Pink

Mylar® or piece of fairly stiff plastic (optional)

HOOK AND EQUIPMENT

3.25mm (US size D/3) crochet hook

Locking or ring stitch marker

Yarn needle

FINISHED MEASUREMENTS

Toothbrush: 2.5 x 11.5cm (1 x 4½in)

Toothpaste: 4 x 11cm (1½ x 4¼in)

ABBREVIATIONS

See page 126

TOOTHBRUSH HANDLE

Using Denim Blue, make a magic ring.

Round 1: 8dc into ring. (*8 sts*)
PM at start of round.

Rounds 2–30: 1dc in each st.
At end of Round 30, sl st in first st to join.
Stuff firmly.
(Optional: Instead of stuffing, insert two or three lolly/popsicle sticks.)
Fasten off.
Cut yarn, thread tail into a yarn needle and close opening by weaving through front loops only.

BRISTLES

Using White, make a magic ring.

Round 1: 8dc into ring. (*8 sts*)
PM at start of round.

Rounds 2–10: 1dc in each st.
Position safety eyes at centre front of bristles, evenly spaced, and fasten securely (see page 124).
Sew face details using Perlé cotton and yarn needle, using Black for V-shaped mouth and Pink for cheeks (see page 125). Fasten off and secure all thread ends.
Add toy stuffing.
Fasten off and cut yarn, leaving a long tail for sewing, thread tail into a yarn needle and close opening by weaving through front loops only.

TOOTHPASTE TUBE

Using White, make a magic ring.

Round 1: 6dc into ring. (*6 sts*)
PM at start of round.

Round 2: 1dcBLO in each st.

Round 3: 1dc in each st.

Round 4: [Inv inc in next st] 6 times. (*12 sts*)

Round 5: [1dc in next st, inv inc in next st] 6 times. (*18 sts*)

Round 6: [1dc in next 2 sts, inv inc in next st] 6 times. (*24 sts*)

Round 7: [1dc in next 3 sts, inv inc in next st] 6 times. (*30 sts*)
Weave in end from magic ring (see page 124).

Round 8: 1dcBLO in each st.
(Optional: Cut a circle of Mylar® or fairly stiff plastic to correspond to top section and insert before cont.)

Round 9: [1dc in next 3 sts, inv dec] 6 times. (*24 sts*)

Round 10: 1dc in each st.
Fasten off White and join in Dark Turquoise.

Rounds 11–13: 1dc in each st.
Join in Light Turquoise.

Round 14: Using Light Turquoise, 1dc in each st.

Round 15: Using Dark Turquoise, 1dc in each st.

Rounds 16–24: Using Light Turquoise, 1dc in each st.

Position safety eyes at centre front of tube, evenly spaced, and fasten securely.
Sew face details using Perlé cotton and yarn needle, using Black for V-shaped mouth and Pink for cheeks. Fasten off and secure all thread ends.
Beg filling with small pieces of toy stuffing, cont adding as body is worked.

Round 25: Using Dark Turquoise, 1dc in each st.

Round 26: Using Light Turquoise, 1dc in each st.
Fasten off Light Turquoise.

Rounds 27–29: Using Dark Turquoise, 1dc in each st.
Fasten off Dark Turquoise and join in White.

Rounds 30–32: 1dc in each st.
Add final toy stuffing as needed.
Fasten off, leaving a long tail for sewing.

MAKING UP AND FINISHING

Place bristles onto toothbrush, with face detail uppermost and use yarn tail to secure into place (see page 124). Fasten off and bury all tails.
Flatten end of toothpaste tube and join with 1dc in each corresponding pair of sts across, working through 2 sts (front and back) to seal end. Fasten off and bury all tails.

CANDLE

Add some cottage-core with this cosy candle character. Topped off with a glowing flame, he is ideal for setting the mood.

SKILL RATING ● ● ○

YARN AND MATERIALS

Cotton DK yarn (100% cotton)
  Orange
  Yellow
  Parchment
  Gold
Toy stuffing
Mylar® or piece of fairly stiff plastic (optional)
Pair of 5–6mm (⅜–¼in) safety eyes
Perlé Cotton No.8 in Black and Pink
Plastic filling pellets (optional)

HOOK AND EQUIPMENT

3.25mm (US size D/3) crochet hook
Locking or ring stitch marker
Yarn needle

FINISHED MEASUREMENTS

6 x 12.5cm (2¼ x 5in)

ABBREVIATIONS

See page 126

CANDLE FLAME

Using Orange, make a magic ring.
Round 1: 4dc into ring. (*4 sts*)
PM at start of round.
Round 2: [1dc in next st, inv inc in next st] twice. (*6 sts*)
Round 3: [1dc in next 2 sts, inv inc in next st] twice. (*8 sts*)
Round 4: [1dc in next st, inv inc in next st] 4 times. (*12 sts*)
Round 5: [1dc in next st, inv inc in next st] 6 times. (*18 sts*)
Weave in end from magic ring (see page 124).
Round 6: 1dc in each st.
Round 7: [1dc in next 2 sts, inv inc in next st] 6 times. (*24 sts*)
Join in Yellow.
Round 8: [3dc in Orange, 1dc in Yellow] 6 times.

Round 9: [2dc in Orange, 2dc in Yellow] 6 times.

Round 10: [1dc in Orange, 3dc in Yellow] 6 times.

Fasten off Orange.

Round 11: 1dc in each st.

Beg filling with small pieces of toy stuffing, cont adding as dec rounds are worked.

Round 12: [1dc in next st, inv dec] 8 times. (*16 sts*)

Round 13: [1dc in next 2 sts, inv dec] 4 times. (*12 sts*)

Add final toy stuffing as needed.

Round 14: [Inv dec] 6 times. (*6 sts*)

Fasten off and cut yarn, leaving a long tail for sewing, thread tail into a yarn needle and close opening by weaving through front loops only.

CANDLE

Using Parchment, make a magic ring.

Round 1: 6dc into ring. (*6 sts*)

PM at start of round.

Round 2: [Inv inc in next st] 6 times. (*12 sts*)

Round 3: [1dc in next st, inv inc in next st] 6 times. (*18 sts*)

Round 4: [1dc in next 2 sts, inv inc in next st] 6 times. (*24 sts*)

Round 5: [1dc in next 3 sts, inv inc in next st] 6 times. (*30 sts*)

Weave in end from magic ring.

Round 6: 1dcBLO in each st.

(Optional: Cut a circle of Mylar® or fairly stiff plastic to correspond to top section and insert before cont.)

Rounds 7–18: 1dc in each st.

Fasten off, leaving a long tail for sewing.

Position safety eyes at centre front of candle, evenly spaced, and fasten securely (see page 124). Sew face details using Perlé cotton and yarn needle, using Black for V-shaped mouth and Pink for cheeks (see page 125). Fasten off and secure all thread ends.

CANDLE HOLDER

Using Gold, make a magic ring.

Round 1: 6dc into ring. (*6 sts*)

PM at start of round.

Round 2: [Inv inc in next st] 6 times. (*12 sts*)

Round 3: [1dc in next st, inv inc in next st] 6 times. (*18 sts*)

Round 4: [1dc in next 2 sts, inv inc in next st] 6 times. (*24 sts*)

Round 5: [1dc in next 3 sts, inv inc in next st] 6 times. (*30 sts*)

Weave in end from magic ring.

Round 6: 1dcBLO in each st.

(Optional: Cut a circle of Mylar® or fairly stiff plastic to correspond to base section and insert before cont.)

Rounds 7–9: 1dc in each st.

Rounds 10 and 11: 1dcFLO in each st.

At end of Round 11, sl st in first st to join.

Fasten off.

MAKING UP AND FINISHING

Place flame onto top of candle and sew into place using yarn tails (see page 124).

(Optional: Insert small bag of plastic filling pellets into base of candle holder and fill rem section with stuffing.)

Stuff the candle firmly.

Working in unworked back loops of candle holder, use yarn tail to sew candle into holder. Before finishing seam add additional stuffing to prevent join section becoming floppy.

Fasten off and bury all tails.

CHAPTER 5

SUPERSIZE

STARFISH

This cheeky sea star is surprisingly simple to make with five repeated arms – you'll want to make a whole prickle of starfish before you know it!

SKILL RATING ● ● ○

YARN AND MATERIALS

Chenille chunky yarn (100% polyester)
   2 balls of Yellow
   Small amounts of Pink and Black
Pair of 12mm (½in) safety eyes
Toy stuffing

HOOK AND EQUIPMENT

6mm (US size J/10) crochet hook
Locking or ring stitch marker
Yarn needle

FINISHED MEASUREMENTS

30.5 x 30.5cm (12 x 12in)

ABBREVIATIONS

See page 126

ARMS

(make 5)
Using Yellow, make a magic ring.
Round 1: 4dc into ring. (*4 sts*)
PM at start of round.
Round 2: [1dc in next st, inv inc in next st] twice. (*6 sts*)
Round 3: 1dc in each st.
Round 4: [1dc in next 2 sts, inv inc in next st] twice. (*8 sts*)

Round 5: 1dc in each st.

Round 6: [1dc in next 3 sts, inv inc in next st] twice. (*10 sts*)

Round 7: 1dc in each st.

Round 8: [1dc in next 4 sts, inv inc in next st] twice. (*12 sts*)

Round 9: 1dc in each st.

Round 10: [1dc in next 5 sts, inv inc in next st] twice. (*14 sts*)

Round 11: [1dc in next 6 sts, inv inc in next st] twice. (*16 sts*)

Round 12: [1dc in next 7 sts, inv inc in next st] twice. (*18 sts*)

Round 13: [1dc in next 8 sts, inv inc in next st] twice. (*20 sts*)

Fasten off first 4 arms, leaving a long tail for sewing, but do not fasten off 5th arm.

CENTRE

Cont from 5th arm, *place next arm alongside, 1dc in each of 10 sts along front; rep from * to add each arm in turn.

Once all arms are joined, sl st between first and 5th arm to join into a ring. (*50 sts*)

Round 1: [1dc in next 4 sts, inv dec] 3 times, [1dc in next 5 sts, inv dec] twice, [1dc in next 4 sts, inv dec] 3 times. (*42 sts*)

Round 2: [1dc in next 5 sts, inv dec] 6 times. (*36 sts*)

Round 3: [1dc in next 4 sts, inv dec] 6 times. (*30 sts*)

Round 4: [1dc in next 3 sts, inv dec] 6 times. (*24 sts*)

Round 5: [1dc in next 2 sts, inv dec] 6 times. (*18 sts*)

Round 6: [1dc in next st, inv dec] 6 times. (*12 sts*)

Round 7: Inv dec in each st. (*6 sts*)

Fasten off and cut yarn, thread tail into a yarn needle and close opening by weaving through front loops only.

Position safety eyes at centre of first side, evenly spaced, and fasten securely (see page 124).

Sew face details using chenille in yarn needle, using Pink for cheeks and Black for V-shaped mouth (see page 125). Fasten off securely. Stuff arms with small pieces of toy stuffing to fill firmly.

BACK OF STARFISH

With WS uppermost join yarn to work second side. Work 1dc in 10 remaining sts of each arm in turn, ending with a sl st between first and 5th arm to join into a ring. (*50 sts*)

Round 1: [1dc in next 4 sts, inv dec] 3 times, [1dc in next 5 sts, inv dec] twice, [1dc in next 4 sts, inv dec] 3 times. (*42 sts*)

Round 2: [1dc in next 5 sts, inv dec] 6 times. (*36 sts*)

Beg filling with small pieces of toy stuffing, cont adding as dec rounds are worked.

Round 3: [1dc in next 4 sts, inv dec] 6 times. (*30 sts*)

Round 4: [1dc in next 3 sts, inv dec] 6 times. (*24 sts*)

Round 5: [1dc in next 2 sts, inv dec] 6 times. (*18 sts*)

Round 6: [1dc in next st, inv dec] 6 times. (*12 sts*)

Add final toy stuffing as needed.

Round 7: [Inv dec] 6 times. (*6 sts*)

Fasten off and cut yarn, thread tail into a yarn needle and close opening by weaving through front loops only.

MAKING UP AND FINISHING

Fasten off and bury all tails.

WHALE

This whale is the king of the ocean, crocheted in two shades of blue to match the waves.

SKILL RATING ● ○ ○

YARN AND MATERIALS
Chenille chunky yarn (100% polyester)
  1 ball of Dark Blue
  1 ball of Light Blue
Small amounts of Pink and Black
Pair of 12mm (½in) safety eyes

Mylar® or piece of fairly stiff plastic (optional)
Toy stuffing

HOOK AND EQUIPMENT
6mm (US size J/10) crochet hook
Locking or ring stitch marker
Yarn needle

FINISHED MEASUREMENTS
30.5 x 14cm (12 x 5½in)

ABBREVIATIONS
See page 126

HEAD

Using Dark Blue, make a magic ring.
Round 1: 6dc into ring. (*6 sts*)
PM at start of round.
Round 2: [Inv inc in next st] 6 times. (*12 sts*)
Round 3: [1dc in next st, inv inc in next st] 6 times. (*18 sts*)
Round 4: [1dc in next 2 sts, inv inc in next st] 6 times. (*24 sts*)
Round 5: [1dc in next 3 sts, inv inc in next st] 6 times. (*30 sts*)
Round 6: [1dc in next 4 sts, inv inc in next st] 6 times. (*36 sts*)
Round 7: [1dc in next 5 sts, inv inc in next st] 6 times. (*42 sts*)
Round 8: [1dc in next 6 sts, inv inc in next st] 6 times. (*48 sts*)
Weave in end from magic ring (see page 124).
Round 9: [1dc in next 7 sts, inv inc in next st] 6 times. (*54 sts*)
Round 10: [1dc in next 8 sts, inv inc in next st] 6 times. (*60 sts*)
Round 11: [1dc in next 9 sts, inv inc in next st] 6 times. (*66 sts*)
Round 12: [1dc in next 10 sts, inv inc in next st] 6 times. (*72 sts*)
Round 13: [1dc in next 11 sts, inv inc in next st] 6 times. (*78 sts*)
Rounds 14–23: 1dc in each st.
Round 24: [1dc in next 11 sts, inv dec] 6 times. (*72 sts*)
Round 25: [1dc in next 10 sts, inv dec] 6 times. (*66 sts*)
Round 26: Change to Light Blue, 1dc in each st.
Round 27: [1dcBLO in next 9 sts, inv dec] 6 times. (*60 sts*)
Position safety eyes at centre front of head, evenly spaced, and fasten securely (see page 124).
Sew face details using chenille and yarn needle, using Pink for cheeks and Black for V-shaped mouth (see page 125). Fasten off securely.
Round 28: [1dc in next 8 sts, inv dec] 6 times. (*54 sts*)

(Optional: Cut a circle of Mylar® or fairly stiff plastic to correspond to base and insert before cont.)
Beg filling with small pieces of toy stuffing, cont adding as dec rounds are worked.
Round 29: [1dc in next 7 sts, inv dec] 6 times. (*48 sts*)
Round 30: [1dc in next 6 sts, inv dec] 6 times. (*42 sts*)
Round 31: [1dc in next 5 sts, inv dec] 6 times. (*36 sts*)
Round 32: [1dc in next 4 sts, inv dec] 6 times. (*30 sts*)
Round 33: [1dc in next 3 sts, inv dec] 6 times. (*24 sts*)
Round 34: [1dc in next 2 sts, inv dec] 6 times. (*18 sts*)
Round 35: [1dc in next st, inv dec] 6 times. (*12 sts*)
Round 36: [Inv dec] 6 times. (*6 sts*)
Fasten off and cut yarn, leaving a long tail for sewing, thread tail into a yarn needle and close opening by weaving through front loops only.

FINS

(make 2)
Using Dark Blue, make a magic ring.
Round 1: 6dc into ring. (*6 sts*)
PM at start of round.
Round 2: [1dc in next st, inv inc in next st] 3 times. (*9 sts*)
Rounds 3–5: 1dc in each st.
Fasten off, leaving a long tail for sewing.

TAIL FIRST PART

Using Dark Blue, make a magic ring.
Round 1: 6dc into ring. (*6 sts*)
PM at start of round.
Round 2: [Inv inc in next st] 6 times. (*12 sts*)
Rounds 3 and 4: 1dc in each st.
Round 5: [1dc in next 2 sts, inv dec] 3 times. (*9 sts*)
Cut yarn and set aside.

TAIL SECOND PART

Using Dark Blue, make a magic ring.
Round 1: 6dc into ring. (*6 sts*)
PM at start of round.
Round 2: [Inv inc in next st] 6 times. (*12 sts*)
Rounds 3 and 4: 1dc in each st.
Round 5: [1dc in next 2 sts, inv dec] 3 times. (*9 sts*)

JOIN TAIL PARTS
Round 6: Place first part next to second part, 1dc in each of 9 sts around first part, 1dc in each of 9 sts around second part. (*18 sts*)
Round 7: [1dc in next st, inv dec] 6 times. (*12 sts*)
Rounds 8 and 9: 1dc in each st.
Fasten off, leaving a long tail for sewing.

MAKING UP AND FINISHING

Position fins on each side of body and sew in place using yarn tails (see page 124). Position tail onto back of whale and sew into place with yarn tail.

PENCIL

This classic pencil is an everyday hero and is sure
to be top of the class with stationery lovers!

SKILL RATING ● ● ○ ○

YARN AND MATERIALS

Chenille chunky yarn (100%
polyester)
 1 ball of Dark Pink
 1 ball of Grey
 1 ball of Yellow
 1 ball of Light Brown
 Long length of Black
 Small amount of Pink

Pair of 12mm (½in) safety eyes

Mylar® or piece of fairly stiff plastic
(optional)

Toy stuffing

HOOK AND EQUIPMENT

6mm (US size J/10) crochet hook

Locking or ring stitch marker

Yarn needle

FINISHED MEASUREMENTS

11.5 x 38cm (4½ x 15in) tall

ABBREVIATIONS

See page 126

ERASER

Using Dark Pink, make a magic ring.
Round 1: 6dc into ring. (*6 sts*)
PM at start of round.
Round 2: [Inv inc in next st] 6 times.
(*12 sts*)
Round 3: [1dc in next st, inv inc in
next st] 6 times. (*18 sts*)
Round 4: [1dc in next 2 sts, inv inc
in next st] 6 times. (*24 sts*)
Round 5: [1dc in next 3 sts, inv inc
in next st] 6 times. (*30 sts*)
Round 6: [1dc in next 4 sts, inv inc
in next st] 6 times. (*36 sts*)
Weave in end from magic ring (see
page 124).
(Optional: Cut a circle of Mylar® or
fairly stiff plastic to correspond to
end and insert before cont.)
Round 7: [1dc in next 5 sts, inv inc
in next st] 6 times. (*42 sts*)
Round 8: 1dcBLO in each st.
Rounds 9–13: 1dc in each st.
Round 14: Change to Grey, 1dcBLO
in each st.
Round 15: 1dc in each st.
Round 16: Change to Yellow, 1dcBLO
in each st.
Begin stuffing with small pieces
of toy stuffing.
Rounds 17–35: 1dc in each st.
Position safety eyes at centre front
of pencil, evenly spaced, and fasten
securely (see page 124).
Sew face details with chenille in
yarn needle, using Pink for cheeks
and Black for V-shaped mouth
(see page 125). Fasten off securely.

Round 36: Change to Light Brown,
1dcBLO in each st.
Round 37: [1dc in next 5 sts, inv dec]
6 times. (*36 sts*)
Round 38: 1dc in each st.
Round 39: [1dc in next 4 sts, inv dec]
6 times. (*30 sts*)
Round 40: 1dc in each st.
Round 41: [1dc in next 3 sts, inv dec]
6 times. (*24 sts*)
Round 42: 1dc in each st.
Round 43: [1dc in next 2 sts, inv dec]
6 times. (*18 sts*)
Finish stuffing centre section.
(Optional: Cut a circle of Mylar®
or fairly stiff plastic and insert
before cont.)
Round 44: 1dc in each st.
Beg filling with small pieces of toy
stuffing, cont adding as dec rounds
are worked.
Round 45: [1dc in next st, inv dec]
6 times. (*12 sts*)
Round 46: Change to Black, 1dcBLO
in each st.
Round 47: 1dc in each st.
Complete stuffing.
Round 48: [Inv dec] 6 times. (*6 sts*)
Round 49: 1dc in each st.
Fasten off and cut yarn, thread
tail into a yarn needle and close
opening by weaving through front
loops only.

MAKING UP AND FINISHING

Fasten off and bury all tails.

BUMBLE BEE

With his chubby, fuzzy body, this plush bumble bee will make a beeline for your heart!

SKILL RATING ● ○ ○

YARN AND MATERIALS

Chenille chunky yarn (100% polyester)
   1 ball of Yellow
   1 ball of Black
   1 ball of White
   Small amount of Pink
Pair of 12mm (½in) safety eyes
Toy stuffing
Floristry or craft wire (15 gauge/1.5mm)
(optional)

HOOK AND EQUIPMENT

6mm (US size J/10) crochet hook
Locking or ring stitch marker
Yarn needle

FINISHED MEASUREMENTS

34 x 20cm (13½ x 8in)

ABBREVIATIONS

See page 126

HEAD

Using Yellow, make a magic ring.
Round 1: 6dc into ring. (*6 sts*)
PM at start of round.
Round 2: [Inv inc in next st] 6 times. (*12 sts*)
Round 3: [1dc in next st, inv inc in next st] 6 times. (*18 sts*)
Round 4: [1dc in next 2 sts, inv inc in next st] 6 times. (*24 sts*)
Round 5: [1dc in next 3 sts, inv inc in next st] 6 times. (*30 sts*)
Round 6: [1dc in next 4 sts, inv inc in next st] 6 times. (*36 sts*)
Round 7: [1dc in next 5 sts, inv inc in next st] 6 times. (*42 sts*)
Round 8: [1dc in next 6 sts, inv inc in next st] 6 times. (*48 sts*)
Weave in end from magic ring (see page 124).
Round 9: [1dc in next 7 sts, inv inc in next st] 6 times. (*54 sts*)
Round 10: [1dc in next 8 sts, inv inc in next st] 6 times. (*60 sts*)
Rounds 11–15: 1dc in each st.
Position safety eyes at centre front of bee, evenly spaced, and fasten securely (see page 124).
Sew face details with chenille in yarn needle, using Pink for cheeks and Black for V-shaped mouth (see page 125). Fasten off securely.
Rounds 16–20: Change to Black, 1dc in each st.
Beg filling with small pieces of toy stuffing, cont adding as rounds are worked.
Rounds 21–25: Change to Yellow, 1dc in each st.
Rounds 26–30: Change to Black, 1dc in each st.
Rounds 31–35: Change to Yellow, 1dc in each st.
Round 36: [1dc in next 8 sts, inv dec] 6 times. (*54 sts*)
Round 37: [1dc in next 7 sts, inv dec] 6 times. (*48 sts*)

Round 38: [1dc in next 6 sts, inv dec] 6 times. (*42 sts*)
Round 39: [1dc in next 5 sts, inv dec] 6 times. (*36 sts*)
Round 40: [1dc in next 4 sts, inv dec] 6 times. (*30 sts*)
Round 41: Change to Black, [1dc in next 3 sts, inv dec] 6 times. (*24 sts*)
Round 42: [1dc in next 2 sts, inv dec] 6 times. (*18 sts*)
Round 43: [1dc in next st, inv dec] 6 times. (*12 sts*)
Round 44: [Inv dec] 6 times. (*6 sts*)
Complete stuffing.
Fasten off and cut yarn, thread tail into a yarn needle and close opening by weaving through front loops only.

WINGS

(make 2)
Using White, make a magic ring.
Round 1: 6dc into ring. (*6 sts*)
PM at start of round.
Round 2: [Inv inc in next st] 6 times. (*12 sts*)
Round 3: [1dc in next st, inv inc in next st] 6 times. (*18 sts*)
Round 4: [1dc in next 2 sts, inv inc in next st] 6 times. (*24 sts*)
Round 5: [1dc in next 3 sts, inv inc in next st] 6 times. (*30 sts*)
Round 6: 1htrFLO in each st.
Round 7: 1dc in each st.
Fasten off, leaving a long tail for sewing.
(Optional: Feed floristry wire through outer edges of wings and secure.)

MAKING UP AND FINISHING

Place wings onto back of bumble bee and sew into place using yarn tails (see page 124).
Fasten off and bury all tails.

JAMMY BISCUIT

This teatime treat is a classic – worked in soft huggable chenille yarn it will become a fast favourite.

SKILL RATING ● ● ●

YARN AND MATERIALS

Chenille chunky yarn (100% polyester)
   2 balls of Light Brown
   1 ball of Red
   Small amounts of Pink and Black

Pair of 12mm (½in) safety eyes

Toy stuffing

Mylar® or piece of fairly stiff plastic (optional)

HOOK AND EQUIPMENT

6mm (US size J/10) crochet hook

Locking or ring stitch marker

Yarn needle

Pins

FINISHED MEASUREMENTS

29.5 x 9cm (11¾ x 3½in)

ABBREVIATIONS

See page 126

NOTE: If you use Mylar® or fairly stiff plastic, the biscuit will have a solid, flat shape. If you omit the stiffening the biscuit will have a softer, pillow-like finish.

BASE LAYER

Using Light Brown, make a magic ring.
Round 1: 6dc into ring. (*6 sts*) PM at start of round.
Round 2: [Inv inc in next st] 6 times. (*12 sts*)
Round 3: [1dc in next st, inv inc in next st] 6 times. (*18 sts*)
Round 4: [1dc in next 2 sts, inv inc in next st] 6 times. (*24 sts*)
Round 5: [1dc in next 3 sts, inv inc in next st] 6 times. (*30 sts*)
Round 6: [1dc in next 4 sts, inv inc in next st] 6 times. (*36 sts*)
Round 7: [1dc in next 5 sts, inv inc in next st] 6 times. (*42 sts*)
Round 8: [1dc in next 6 sts, inv inc in next st] 6 times. (*48 sts*)
Weave in end from magic ring (see page 124).
Round 9: [1dc in next 7 sts, inv inc in next st] 6 times. (*54 sts*)
Round 10: [1dc in next 8 sts, inv inc in next st] 6 times. (*60 sts*)
Round 11: [1dc in next 9 sts, inv inc in next st] 6 times. (*66 sts*)

Round 12: [1dc in next 10 sts, inv inc in next st] 6 times. (*72 sts*)
Round 13: [1dc in next 11 sts, inv inc in next st] 6 times. (*78 sts*)
Round 14: [1dc in next 12 sts, inv inc in next st] 6 times. (*84 sts*)
Round 15: [1dc in next 13 sts, inv inc in next st] 6 times. (*90 sts*)
Round 16: 1htr in each st.
Round 17: 1dcBLO in each st.
(Optional: Cut two circles of Mylar® or fairly stiff plastic to correspond to base layer and insert one before cont. Set aside second circle.)

SIDE SECTION

Rounds 18 and 19: 1htr in each st.
Round 20: 1dcBLO in each st.

TOP LAYER

Round 21: 1htr in each st.
Round 22: [1dc in next 13 sts, inv dec] 6 times. (*84 sts*)
Round 23: [1dc in next 12 sts, inv dec] 6 times. (*78 sts*)
Round 24: [1dc in next 11 sts, inv dec] 6 times. (*72 sts*)
Round 25: [1dc in next 10 sts, inv dec] 6 times. (*66 sts*)
Round 26: [1dc in next 9 sts, inv dec] 6 times. (*60 sts*)

Round 27: 1dc in next 27 sts, 1htr in next st, 1tr in next st, 1dtr in next st, 1tr in next st, 1htr in next st, 1dc in next 28 sts.

Round 28: [1dc in next 8 sts, inv dec] twice, 1dc in next 7 sts, 1htr in next st, 1tr in next st, 1dtr in next st, 1tr in next st, 1htr in next st, 1dc in next 8 sts, [1dc in next 8 sts, inv dec] twice. (*56 sts*)
Fasten off, leaving a long tail for sewing.

TOP ACCENT
Join Light Brown next to cutout section and work surface sl st around cutout.
Fasten off.

JAMMY CENTRE
Using Red, make a magic ring.
Round 1: 6dc into ring. (*6 sts*)
PM at start of round.
Round 2: [Inv inc in next st] 6 times. (*12 sts*)
Round 3: [1dc in next st, inv inc in next st] 6 times. (*18 sts*)
Round 4: [1dc in next 2 sts, inv inc in next st] 6 times. (*24 sts*)
Round 5: [1dc in next 3 sts, inv inc in next st] 6 times. (*30 sts*)
Round 6: [1dc in next 4 sts, inv inc in next st] 6 times. (*36 sts*)
Round 7: [1dc in next 5 sts, inv inc in next st] 6 times. (*42 sts*)
Round 8: [1dc in next 6 sts, inv inc in next st] 6 times. (*48 sts*)
Weave in end from magic ring.
Round 9: [1dc in next 7 sts, inv inc in next st] 6 times. (*54 sts*)
Round 10: [1dc in next 8 sts, inv inc in next st] 6 times. (*60 sts*)
Round 11: 1dc in each st.
Fasten off, leaving a long tail for sewing.

Position safety eyes at centre front, evenly spaced, and fasten securely (see page 124).
Sew face details using chenille in yarn needle, using Pink for cheeks and Black for V-shaped mouth (see page 125).
Fasten off securely.

MAKING UP AND FINISHING
Stuff centre of biscuit with small sections of toy stuffing until firm. (Optional: Add in second Mylar® circle.)
Insert jammy centre into cutout section of top layer and pin in place. Using yarn tails, secure jammy centre into place (see page 125).
Fasten off and bury all tails.

AVOCADO

Undisputedly the cutest fruit in town, this avocado even has a plump stone in his belly.

SKILL RATING ● ○ ○

YARN AND MATERIALS

Chenille chunky yarn (100% polyester)
 1 ball of Light Brown
 1 ball of Dark Green
 1 ball of Light Green
Small amounts of Pink and Black
Pair of 12mm (½in) safety eyes
Toy stuffing

HOOK AND EQUIPMENT

6mm (US size J/10) crochet hook
Locking or ring stitch marker
Yarn needle

FINISHED MEASUREMENTS

25 x 35.5cm (9¾ x 14in)

ABBREVIATIONS

See page 126

STONE

Using Light Brown, make a magic ring.
Round 1: 8dc into ring. (*8 sts*) PM at start of round.
Round 2: [Inv inc in next st] 8 times. (*16 sts*)
Round 3: [1dc in next st, inv inc in next st] 8 times. (*24 sts*)
Round 4: [1dc in next 2 sts, inv inc in next st] 8 times. (*32 sts*)
Round 5: [1dc in next 3 sts, inv inc in next st] 8 times. (*40 sts*)
Round 6: [1dc in next 4 sts, inv inc in next st] 8 times. (*48 sts*) Weave in end from magic ring (see page 124).
Rounds 7–10: 1dc in each st. Fasten off and set aside.

TOP SECTION

Using Light Green, make a magic ring.
Round 1: 8dc into ring. (*8 sts*) PM at start of round.
Round 2: [Inv inc in next st] 8 times. (*16 sts*)
Round 3: [1dc in next st, inv inc in next st] 8 times. (*24 sts*)
Round 4: [1dc in next 2 sts, inv inc in next st] 8 times. (*32 sts*)
Round 5: [1dc in next 3 sts, inv inc in next st] 8 times. (*40 sts*)
Round 6: [1dc in next 4 sts, inv inc in next st] 8 times. (*48 sts*) Weave in end from magic ring.
Round 7: [1dc in next 5 sts, inv inc in next st] 8 times. (*56 sts*)
Round 8: [1dc in next 6 sts, inv inc in next st] 8 times. (*64 sts*)

Round 9: [1dc in next 7 sts, inv inc in next st] 8 times. (*72 sts*)

Round 10: [1dc in next 8 sts, inv inc in next st] 8 times. (*80 sts*)

Round 11: 1dc in each st.
Beg working in rows.

Row 12: 1htr in next 4 sts, 1dc in next 12 sts, 1htr in next 4 sts, turn. (*20 sts*)
Working back and forth in rows on these 20 sts.

Row 13: Ch1, dc2tog, 1dc in next 16 sts, dc2tog. (*18 sts*)

Row 14: Ch1, 1dc in each st.

Row 15: Ch1, dc2tog, 1dc in next 14 sts, dc2tog. (*16 sts*)

Row 16: Ch1, 1dc in each st.

Row 17: Ch1, dc2tog, 1dc in next 12 sts, dc2tog. (*14 sts*)

Row 18: Ch1, 1dc in each st.

Row 19: Ch1, dc2tog, 1dc in next 10 sts, dc2tog. (*12 sts*)

Row 20: Ch1, 1dc in each st.

Row 21: Ch1, dc2tog, 1dc in next 8 sts, dc2tog. (*10 sts*)

Row 22: Ch1, 1dc in each st.

Row 23: Ch1, dc2tog, 1dc in next 6 sts, dc2tog. (*8 sts*)

Row 24: Ch1, 1dc in each st.

Row 25: Ch1, dc2tog, 1dc in next 4 sts, dc2tog. (*6 sts*)

Row 26: Ch1, dc2tog, 1dc in next 2 sts, dc2tog. (*4 sts*)

BORDER

Round 27: Working around outer edge, 1dc in each st. (*94 sts*)
Fasten off, leaving a long tail for sewing.
Position safety eyes at centre front at top of avocado, evenly spaced, and fasten securely (see page 124). Sew face details with chenille in yarn needle, using Pink for cheeks and Black for V-shaped mouth (see page 125). Fasten off securely.

JOIN IN STONE

Place stone onto corresponding circle of top section and begin sewing into place using yarn tail (see page 124), filling with small pieces of toy stuffing at a time until stone is padded before completely securing.
Fasten off.

LOWER SECTION

Using Dark Green, make a magic ring.

Round 1: 8dc into ring. (*8 sts*)
PM at start of round.

Round 2: [Inv inc in next st] 8 times. (*16 sts*)

Round 3: [1dc in next st, inv inc in next st] 8 times. (*24 sts*)

Round 4: [1dc in next 2 sts, inv inc in next st] 8 times. (*32 sts*)

Round 5: [1dc in next 3 sts, inv inc in next st] 8 times. (*40 sts*)

Round 6: [1dc in next 4 sts, inv inc in next st] 8 times. (*48 sts*)
Weave in end from magic ring.

Round 7: [1dc in next 5 sts, inv inc in next st] 8 times. (*56 sts*)

Round 8: [1dc in next 6 sts, inv inc in next st] 8 times. (*64 sts*)

Round 9: [1dc in next 7 sts, inv inc in next st] 8 times. (*72 sts*)

Round 10: [1dc in next 8 sts, inv inc in next st] 8 times. (*80 sts*)

Round 11: 1dc in each st.
Beg working in rows.

Row 12: 1htr in next 4 sts, 1dc in next 12 sts, 1htr in next 4 sts, turn. (*20 sts*)
Work back and forth in rows on these 20 sts.

Row 13: Ch1, dc2tog, 1dc in next 16 sts, dc2tog. (*18 sts*)

Row 14: Ch1, 1dc in each st.

Row 15: Ch1, dc2tog, 1dc in next 14 sts, dc2tog. (*16 sts*)

Row 16: Ch1, 1dc in each st.

Row 17: Ch1, dc2tog, 1dc in next 12 sts, dc2tog. (*14 sts*)

Row 18: Ch1, 1dc in each st.

Row 19: Ch1, dc2tog, 1dc in next 10 sts, dc2tog. (*12 sts*)

Row 20: Ch1, 1dc in each st.

Row 21: Ch1, dc2tog, 1dc in next 8 sts, dc2tog. (*10 sts*)

Row 22: Ch1, 1dc in each st.

Row 23: Ch1, dc2tog, 1dc in next 6 sts, dc2tog. (*8 sts*)

Row 24: Ch1, 1dc in each st.

Row 25: Ch1, dc2tog, 1dc in next 4 sts, dc2tog. (*6 sts*)

Row 26: Ch1, dc2tog, 1dc in next 2 sts, dc2tog. (*4 sts*)

BORDER

Round 27: Working around outer edge, 1dc in each st. (*94 sts*)

Rounds 28–31: 1dc in each st.

JOIN AVOCADO

Place lighter section on top and join with 1dc in each st through both pieces, using back loops only for upper section. Fill with toy stuffing as you work.
Fasten off.

MAKING UP AND FINISHING

Fasten off and bury all tails.

RACCOON

A woodland character with a friendly face — the monochrome colouring makes him look like a little bandit.

SKILL RATING ● ● ●

YARN AND MATERIALS

Chenille chunky yarn (100% polyester)
  1 ball of White
  1 ball of Black
  1 ball of Light Grey
  Small amounts of Yellow and Pink
Pair of ½in (12mm) safety eyes
Toy stuffing

HOOK AND EQUIPMENT

6mm (US size J/10) crochet hook
Locking or ring stitch marker
Yarn needle
Pins

FINISHED MEASUREMENTS

20 x 34.5cm (8 x 13½in)

ABBREVIATIONS

See page 126

EYES

(make 2)
Using White, make a magic ring.
Round 1: 6dc into ring. (*6 sts*)
PM at start of round.
Round 2: [Inv inc in next st] 6 times. (*12 sts*)
Round 3: [1dc in next st, inv inc in next st] 6 times, join with sl st in first st. (*18 sts*)
Fasten off, leaving a long tail for sewing.
Position safety eye at centre front of each eye and fasten securely (see page 124).
Set aside.

EARS

(make 2)
Using Black, make a magic ring.
Round 1: 5dc into ring. (*5 sts*)
PM at start of round.
Round 2: 1dc in next 4 sts, inv inc in next st. (*6 sts*)
Round 3: [1dc in next st, inv inc in next st] 3 times. (*9 sts*)
Round 4: [1dc in next 2 sts, inv inc in next st] 3 times. (*12 sts*)
Rounds 5 and 6: 1dc in each st.
Fasten off, leaving a long tail for sewing.

HEAD

Using Light Grey, make a magic ring.
Round 1: 6dc into ring. (*6 sts*)
PM at start of round.
Round 2: [Inv inc in next st] 6 times. (*12 sts*)
Round 3: [1dc in next st, inv inc in next st] 6 times. (*18 sts*)
Round 4: [1dc in next 2 sts, inv inc in next st] 6 times. (*24 sts*)
Round 5: [1dc in next 3 sts, inv inc in next st] 6 times. (*30 sts*)
Round 6: [1dc in next 4 sts, inv inc in next st] 6 times. (*36 sts*)
Round 7: [1dc in next 5 sts, inv inc in next st] 6 times. (*42 sts*)
Round 8: [1dc in next 6 sts, inv inc in next st] 6 times. (*48 sts*)
Weave in end from magic ring (see page 124).
Rounds 9–15: Change to Black, 1dc in each st.
Rounds 16 and 17: Change to White, 1dc in each st.
Position ears on top of head, sew in place using yarn tails (see page 124).
Position eyes, sew in place using yarn tails.
Sew face details using chenille in yarn needle, using Pink for cheeks and Black for V-shaped mouth (see page 125). Fasten off securely.

Round 18: [1dc in next 6 sts, inv dec] 6 times. (*42 sts*)
Beg filling with small pieces of toy stuffing, cont adding as dec rounds are worked.
Round 19: [1dc in next 5 sts, inv dec] 6 times. (*36 sts*)
Round 20: [1dc in next 4 sts, inv dec] 6 times. (*30 sts*)
Round 21: [1dc in next 3 sts, inv dec] 6 times. (*24 sts*)
Round 22: [1dc in next 2 sts, inv dec] 6 times. (*18 sts*)
Add final toy stuffing as needed.
Round 23: [1dc in next st, inv dec] 6 times. (*12 sts*)
Fasten off, leaving a long tail for sewing.

ARMS

(make 2)
Using Black, make a magic ring.
Round 1: 6dc into ring. (*6 sts*)
PM at start of round.
Round 2: [Inv inc in next st] 6 times. (*12 sts*)
Round 3: 1dc in each st.
Round 4: 1dc in next 10 sts, inv dec. (*11 sts*)
Round 5: 1dc in next 9 sts, inv dec. (*10 sts*)
Rounds 6–8: Change to White, 1dc in each st.
Rounds 9–12: Change to Black, 1dc in each st.
Rounds 13–17: Change to White, 1dc in each st.
Fasten off, leaving a long tail for sewing.

FIRST LEG

Using Black, make a magic ring.
Round 1: 6dc into ring. (*6 sts*)
PM at start of round.
Round 2: [Inv inc in next st] 6 times. (*12 sts*)
Weave in end from magic ring.
Round 3: [1dc in next st, inv inc in next st] 6 times. (*18 sts*)
Rounds 4–8: Change to Light Grey, 1dc in each st.
Fasten off and set aside.

SECOND LEG

Using Black, make a magic ring.
Round 1: 6dc into ring. (*6 sts*)
PM at start of round.
Round 2: [Inv inc in next st] 6 times. (*12 sts*)
Weave in end from magic ring.
Round 3: [1dc in next st, inv inc in next st] 6 times. (*18 sts*)
Rounds 4–8: Change to Light Grey, 1dc in each st.
Do not fasten off.

JOIN LEGS

Round 9: Place first leg next to second leg, 1dc in each of 18 sts around first leg, 1dc in each of 18 sts around second leg. (*36 sts*)

BANDANA

Using Yellow, ch3.

Row 1: Beg in 2nd st from hook, 1dc in each ch to end. (*2 sts*)

Row 2: Ch1, inv inc in each st. (*4 sts*)

Row 3: Ch1, inv inc in next st, 1dc in next 2 sts, inv inc in next st. (*6 sts*)

Row 4: Ch1, inv inc in next st, 1dc in next 4 sts, inv inc in next st. (*8 sts*)

Row 5: Ch1, inv inc in next st, 1dc in next 6 sts, inv inc in next st. (*10 sts*)

Row 6: Ch1, inv inc in next st, 1dc in next 8 sts, inv inc in next st. (*12 sts*)

Row 7: Ch1, inv inc in next st, 1dc in next 10 sts, inv inc in next st, ch12. (*14 sts*)

Fasten off, leaving a long tail for sewing.

BODY

Rounds 10–16: 1dc in each st.

Beg filling with small pieces of toy stuffing, cont adding as dec rounds are worked.

Round 17: [1dc in next 4 sts, inv dec] 6 times. (*30 sts*)

Rounds 18 and 19: 1dc in each st.

Round 20: [1dc in next 3 sts, inv dec] 6 times. (*24 sts*)

Round 21: 1dc in each st.

Round 22: [1dc in next 2 sts, inv dec] 6 times. (*18 sts*)

Add final toy stuffing as needed.

Round 23: [1dc in next st, inv dec] 6 times. (*12 sts*)

Fasten off, leaving a long tail for sewing.

TAIL

Using Black, make a magic ring.

Round 1: 6dc into ring. (*6 sts*) PM at start of round.

Round 2: [1dc in next st, inv inc in next st] 3 times. (*9 sts*)

Round 3: 1dc in each st.

Round 4: [1dc in next 2 sts, inv inc in next st] 3 times. (*12 sts*)

Round 5: Change to White, 1dc in each st.

Round 6: [1dc in next 2 sts, inv inc in next st] 4 times. (*16 sts*)

Round 7: 1dc in each st.

Round 8: [1dc in next 2 sts, inv dec] 4 times. (*12 sts*)

Rounds 9–12: Change to Black, 1dc in each st.

Round 13: Change to White, [1dc in next 2 sts, inv dec] 3 times. (*9 sts*)

Rounds 14–17: 1dc in each st.

Round 18: [1dc in next st, inv dec] 3 times. (*6 sts*)

Fasten off, leaving a long tail for sewing.

MAKING UP AND FINISHING

Stuff arms lightly, pin onto sides of body. Place head onto body and sew in place using yarn tails, working through stitches around neck section (see page 124). While working around ensure that upper sections of arms are secured into seam. Before working final stitches add in any additional toy stuffing to neck section to prevent it becoming floppy.

Tie bandana around neck and secure with yarn tail.

Fasten off and bury all tails.

TECHNIQUES

In this section, you'll find all the simple crochet and finishing techniques that you'll need to make the projects in this book.

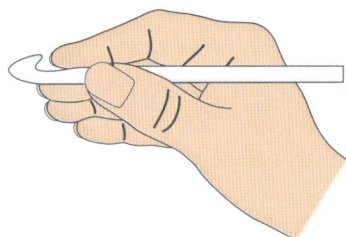

Holding the hook

Pick up your hook as though you are picking up a pen or pencil. Keeping the hook held loosely between your fingers and thumb, turn your hand so that the palm is facing up and the hook is balanced in your hand and resting in the space between your index finger and your thumb.

You can also hold the hook like a knife – this may be easier if you are working with a large hook or with chunky yarn. Choose the method that you find most comfortable.

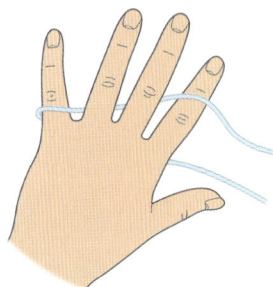

Holding the yarn

1 Pick up the yarn with your little finger in the opposite hand to your hook, with your palm facing upwards and with the short end in front. Turn your hand to face downwards, with the yarn on top of your index finger and under the other two fingers and wrapped right around the little finger, as shown above.

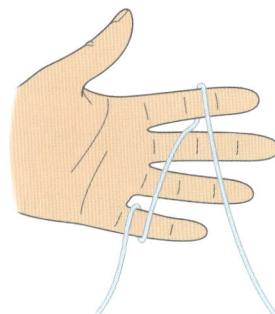

2 Turn your hand to face you, ready to hold the work in your middle finger and thumb. Keeping your index finger only at a slight curve, hold the work or the slip knot using the same hand, between your middle finger and your thumb and just below the crochet hook and loop/s on the hook.

Holding the hook and yarn while crocheting

Keep your index finger, with the yarn draped over it, at a slight curve, and hold your work (or the slip knot) using the same hand, between your middle finger and your thumb and just below the crochet hook and loop/s on the hook.

As you draw the loop through the hook release the yarn on the index finger to allow the loop to stay loose on the hook. If you tense your index finger, the yarn will become too tight and pull the loop on the hook too tight for you to draw the yarn through.

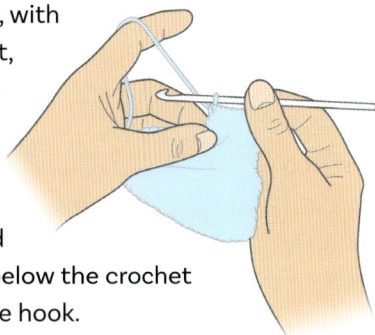

Holding the hook and yarn for left-handers

Some left-handers learn to crochet like right-handers, but others learn with everything reversed – with the hook in the left hand and the yarn in the right.

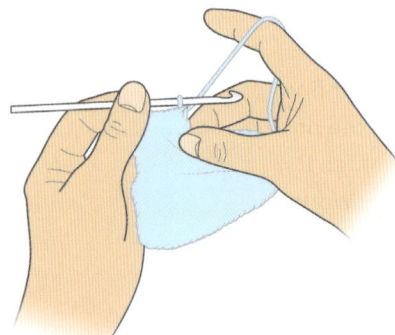

Making a slip knot

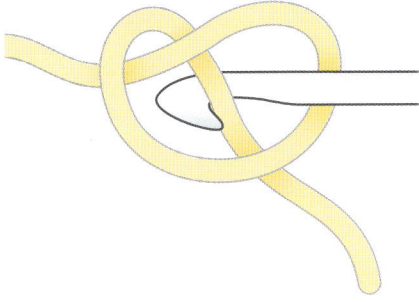

1 In one hand hold the circle at the top where the yarn crosses, and let the tail drop down at the back so that it falls across the centre of the loop. With your free hand or the tip of a crochet hook, pull a loop through the circle.

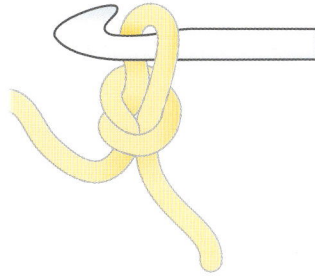

2 Put the hook into the loop and pull gently so that it forms a loose loop on the hook.

Yarn round hook

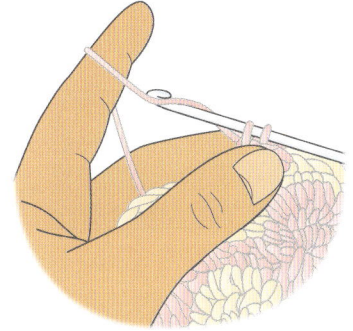

To create a stitch, catch the yarn from behind with the hook pointing upwards. As you gently pull the yarn through the loop on the hook, turn the hook so it faces downwards and slide the yarn through the loop. The loop on the hook should be kept loose enough for the hook to slide through easily.

Magic ring

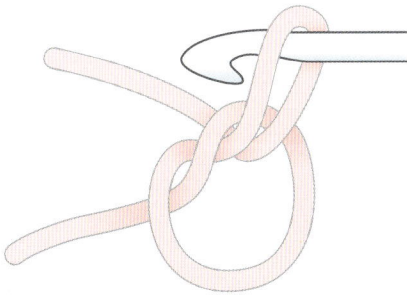

This is a useful starting technique if you do not want a visible hole in the centre of your round. Loop the yarn around your finger, insert the hook through the ring, yarn round hook, pull through the ring to make the first chain. Work the number of stitches required into the ring and then pull the end to tighten the centre ring and close the hole.

Chain

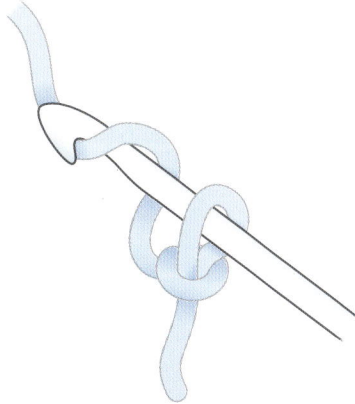

1 Using the hook, wrap the yarn round the hook ready to pull it through the loop on the hook.

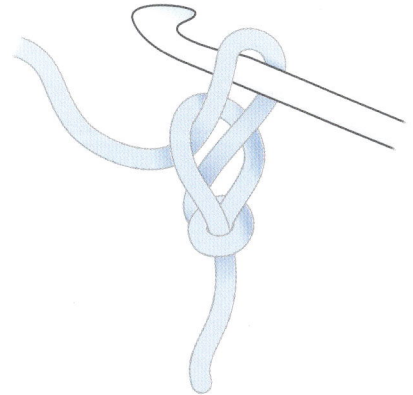

2 Pull through, creating a new loop on the hook. Continue in this way to create a chain of the required length.

Slip stitch (sl st)

A slip stitch doesn't create any height and is often used as the last stitch to create a smooth and even round or row.

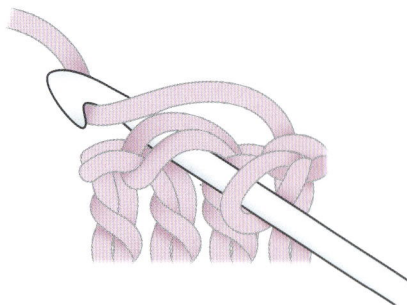

1 To make a slip stitch: first put the hook through the work, yarn round hook.

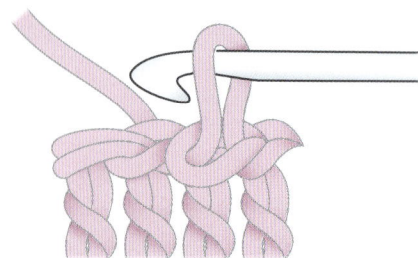

2 Pull the yarn through both the work and through the loop on the hook at the same time, so you will have 1 loop on the hook.

Continuous spiral

After completing the base ring, place a stitch marker in the first stitch and then continue to crochet around. When you have made a round and reached the point where the stitch marker is, work this stitch, take out the stitch marker from the previous round and put it back into the first stitch of the new round. A safety pin or piece of yarn in a contrasting colour makes a good stitch marker.

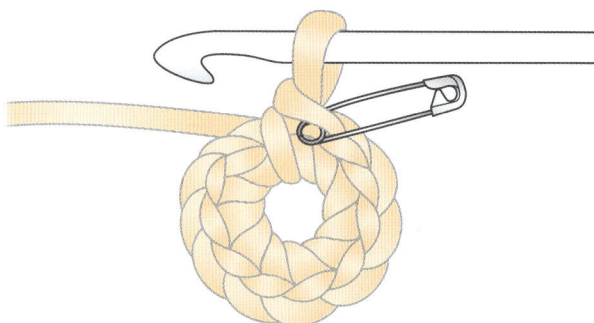

Working into top of stitch

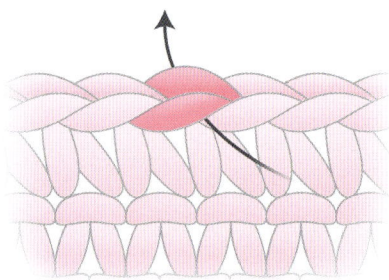

Unless otherwise directed, always insert the hook under both of the two loops on top of the stitch – this is the standard technique.

Working into front loop of stitch (FLO)

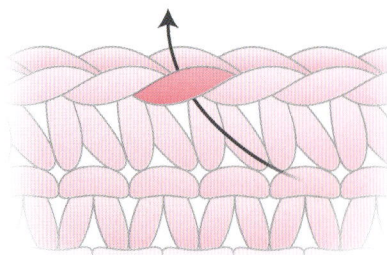

To work into the front loop of a stitch, pick up the front loop from underneath at the front of the work.

Working into back loop of stitch (BLO)

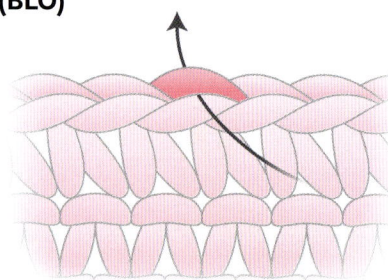

To work into the back loop of the stitch, insert the hook between the front and the back loop, picking up the back loop from the front of the work.

Double crochet (dc)

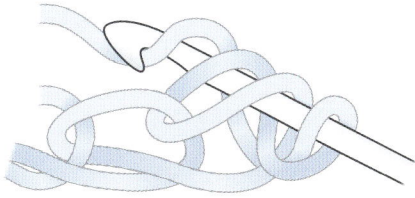

1 Insert the hook into your work, yarn round hook and pull the yarn through the work only. You will then have 2 loops on the hook.

2 Yarn round hook again and pull through the 2 loops on the hook. You will then have 1 loop on the hook.

Half treble crochet (htr)

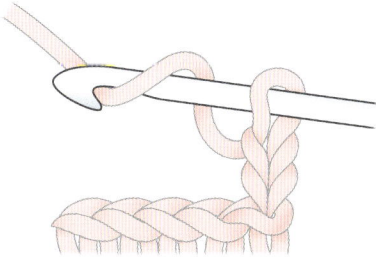

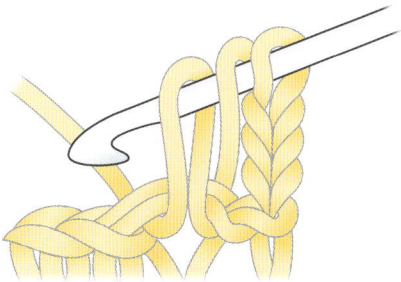

1 Before inserting the hook into the work, wrap the yarn round the hook and put the hook through the work with the yarn wrapped around.

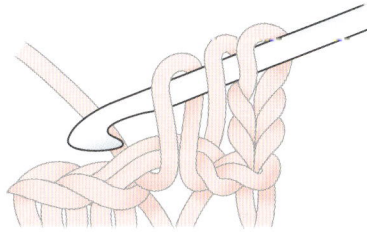

2 Yarn round hook again and pull through the first loop on the hook. You now have 3 loops on the hook.

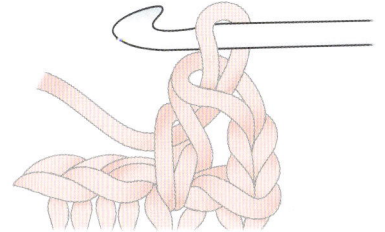

3 Yarn round hook and pull the yarn through all 3 loops. You will be left with 1 loop on the hook.

Treble crochet (tr)

1 Before inserting the hook into the work, wrap the yarn round the hook. Put the hook through the work with the yarn wrapped around, yarn round hook again and pull through the first loop on the hook. You now have 3 loops on the hook.

2 Yarn round hook again, pull the yarn through the first 2 loops on the hook. You now have 2 loops on the hook.

3 Pull the yarn through 2 loops again. You will be left with 1 loop on the hook.

Double treble crochet (dtr)

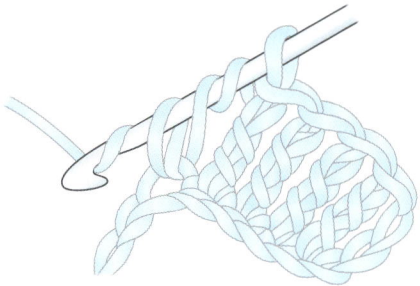

Yarn round hook twice, insert the hook into the stitch, yarn round hook, pull a loop through (4 loops on hook), yarn round hook, pull the yarn through 2 stitches (3 loops on hook), yarn round hook, pull a loop through the next 2 stitches (2 loops on hook), yarn round hook, pull a loop through the last 2 stitches. You will be left with 1 loop on the hook.

Increasing

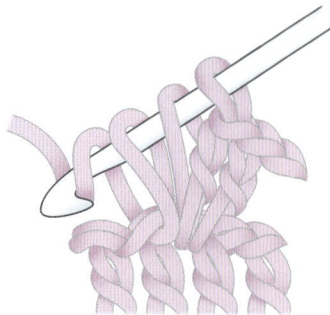

Make two or three stitches into one stitch or space from the previous row. The illustration shows a treble crochet increase being made.

Decreasing

You can decrease by either missing the next stitch and continuing to crochet, or by crocheting two or more stitches together. The basic technique for crocheting stitches together is the same, no matter which stitch you are using.

Double crochet two stitches together (dc2tog)

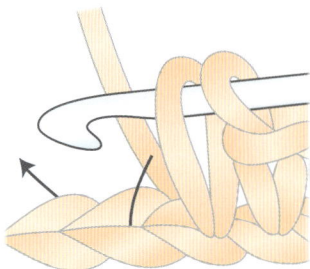

1 Insert the hook into your work, yarn round hook and pull the yarn through the work (2 loops on hook). Insert the hook in next stitch, yarn round hook and pull the yarn through.

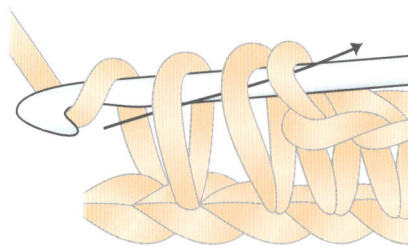

2 Yarn round hook again and pull through all 3 loops on the hook. You will then have 1 loop on the hook.

Joining yarn

You can use this technique when changing colour, or when joining in a new ball of yarn as one runs out.

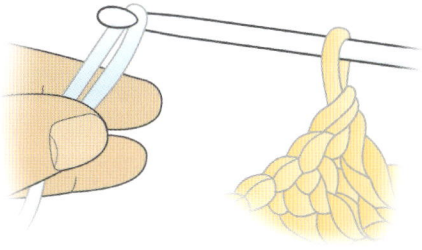

1 Keep the loop of the old yarn on the hook. Drop the tail and catch a loop of the strand of the new yarn with the crochet hook and pull the yarn through.

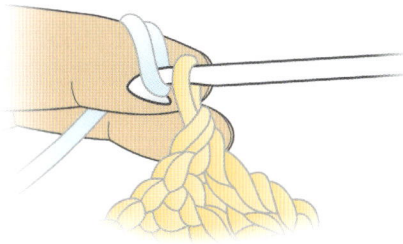

2 Draw the new yarn through the loop on the hook, keeping the old loop drawn tight and continue as instructed in the pattern.

Enclosing a yarn tail

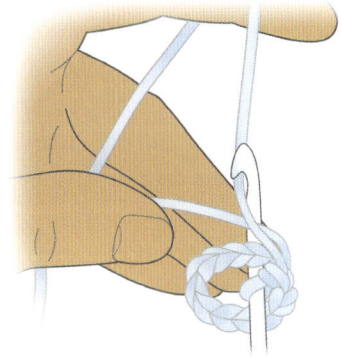

You may find that the yarn tail gets in the way as you work; you can enclose this into the stitches as you go by placing the tail at the back as you wrap the yarn. This also saves having to sew this tail end in later.

Fastening off

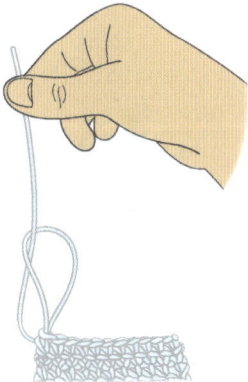

When you have finished crocheting, you need to fasten off the stitches to stop all your work unravelling. Draw up the final loop of the last stitch to make it bigger. Cut the yarn, leaving a tail of approximately 10cm (4in) – unless a longer end is needed for sewing up. Pull the tail all the way through the loop and pull the loop up tightly.

Joining in new yarn after fastening off

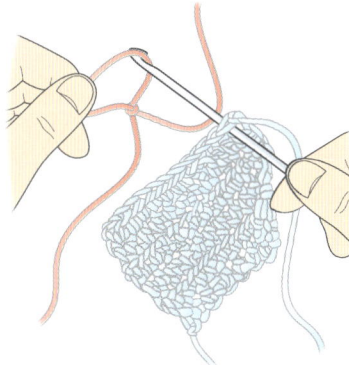

1 Fasten off the old colour (see left). Make a slip knot with the new colour (see page 119). Insert the hook into the stitch at the beginning of the next row, then through the slip knot.

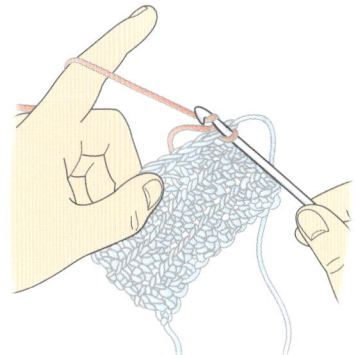

2 Draw the loop of the slip knot through to the front of the work. Carry on working using the new colour, following the instructions in the pattern.

Special amigurumi stitches

Invisible increase (inv inc)
This adds an extra stitch without making a hole in the crochet fabric. Work 2 double crochet in the same stitch but the first stitch is worked through the front loop only and the second stitch is worked through the whole stitch (front and back loops as for a standard double crochet).

Invisible decrease (inv dec)
A decrease that reduces a stitch without making a hole in the crochet fabric. The next 2 stitches are worked together to make one double crochet, the stitch is worked through the front loops only of both stitches.

Invisible colour change (inv colour change)
Work the last stitch of previous colour though the back loop only. Make a slip knot with the new yarn, chain 1 and work 1 double crochet in same stitch and continue in new colour.

Weaving in yarn ends

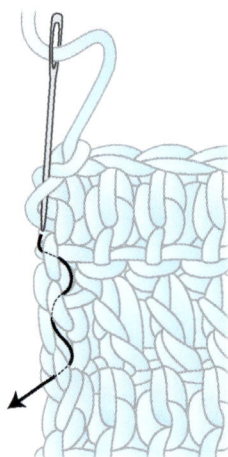

It is important to weave in the tail ends of the yarn so that they are secure and your crochet won't unravel. Thread a yarn needle with the tail end of yarn. On the wrong side, take the needle through the crochet one stitch down on the edge, then take it through the stitches, working in a gentle zigzag. Work through 4 or 5 stitches then return in the opposite direction. Remove the needle, pull the crochet gently to stretch it and trim the end.

Sewing seams

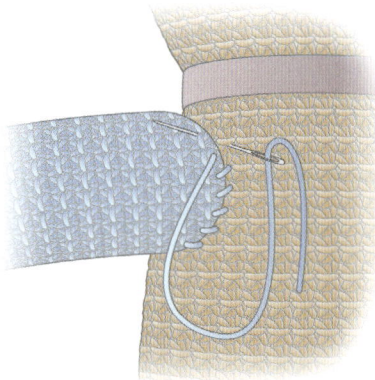

Thread a needle with the yarn end from the piece you are attaching. Use whip stitch to sew the pieces together, catching the end of the piece to be attached and then picking up the nearest stitch on the main piece. Continue until the pieces are securely sewn together, then fasten off and lose the yarn end inside one of the stuffed pieces.

Adding safety eyes

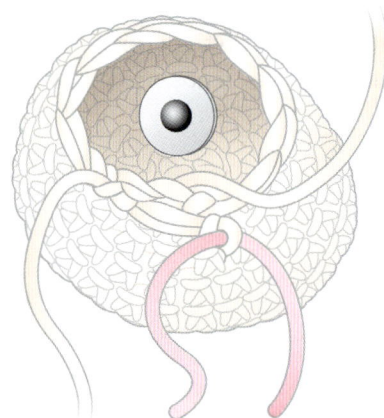

Insert each eye from the front and make sure both eyes are completely level and sitting on the same round before you secure the safety catches at the back. The flat piece of the safety catch is pushed towards the crochet piece from the inside.

A safety eye insertion tool will make fitting the eyes easier. This usually consists of a piece of metal or plastic with holes for extra leverage when securing the eye washers.

Straight stitch

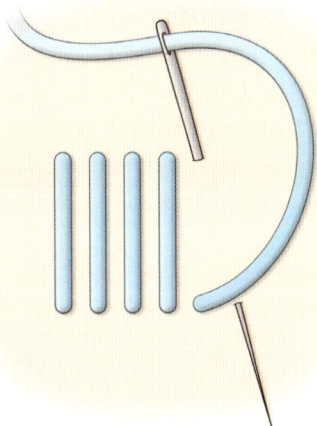

These stitches are used for the mouth and cheek details. Bring the needle through to the surface of the fabric and then take it back down to create a small straight stitch.

Tassels and fringes

Tassels are single clusters of lark's head knots; if they are repeated close together along an edge this creates a fringe. Use the same colour yarn as for your project, or choose a contrasting colour of your choice.

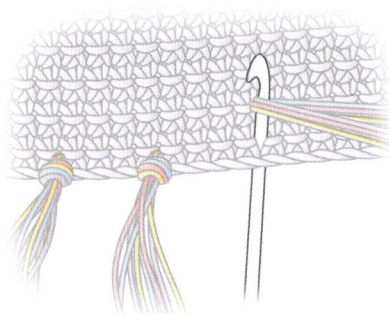

1 Cut strands of yarn to the length given in the pattern. Take one or more strands and fold in half. With the right side of the project facing, insert a crochet hook in one of the edge stitches from the wrong side. Catch the bunch of strands with the hook at the fold point.

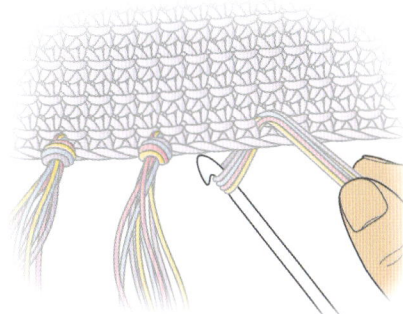

2 Draw all the loops through the stitch.

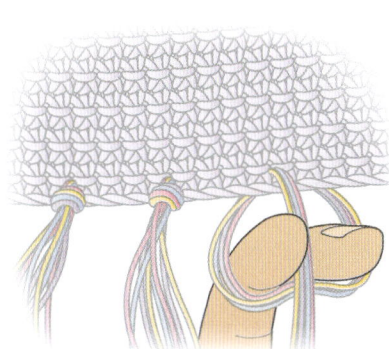

3 Pull through to make a big loop and, using your fingers, pull the tails of the bunch of strands through the loop.

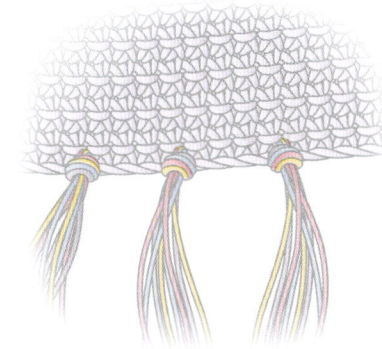

4 Pull on the tails to tighten the loop firmly to secure the tassel.

Making a double crochet seam

With a double crochet seam you join two pieces together using a crochet hook and working a double crochet stitch through both pieces, instead of sewing them together with a tail of yarn and a yarn sewing needle. This makes a quick and strong seam and gives a slightly raised finish to the edging. For a less raised seam, follow the same basic technique, but work each stitch in slip stitch rather than double crochet.

1 Start by lining up the two pieces with wrong sides together. Insert the hook in the top 2 loops of the stitch of the first piece, then into the corresponding stitch on the second piece.

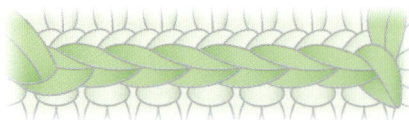

2 Complete the double crochet stitch as normal and continue on the next stitches as directed in the pattern. This gives a raised effect if the double crochet stitches are made on the right side of the work.

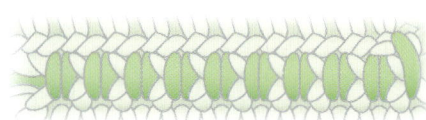

3 You can work with the wrong side of the work facing (with the pieces right side facing) if you don't want this effect and it still creates a good strong join.

Crochet Stitch Conversion Chart

Crochet stitches are worked in the same way in both the UK and the USA, but the stitch names are not the same and identical names are used for different stitches. Below is a list of the UK terms used in this book, and the equivalent US terms.

UK TERM	US TERM
double crochet (dc)	single crochet (sc)
half treble (htr)	half double crochet (hdc)
treble (tr)	double crochet (dc)
double treble (dtr)	treble (tr)
tension	gauge
yarn round hook (yrh)	yarn over hook (yoh)

Abbreviations (UK terms)

beg	begin(ning)
BLO	back loop only
ch	chain
cont	continu(e)ing
dc	double crochet
dec	decrease
dtr	double treble crochet
FLO	front loop only
htr	half treble crochet
inc	increase
inv	invisible (see page 124)
opp	opposite
PM	place marker
sl st	slip stitch
st(s)	stitch(es)
rep	repeat
RS	right side
tr	treble crochet
WS	wrong side
yrh	yarn round hook

Index

Suppliers

UK

LoveCrafts
Online sales
www.lovecrafts.com

Wool
Yarn, hooks
Store in Bath
+44 (0)1225 469144
www.woolbath.co.uk

Wool Warehouse
Online sales
www.woolwarehouse.co.uk

Laughing Hens
Online sales
Tel: +44 (0) 1829 740903
www.laughinghens.com

John Lewis
Yarns and craft supplies
Telephone numbers of
stores on website
www.johnlewis.com

Hobbycraft
Yarns and craft supplies
www.hobbycraft.co.uk

USA

LoveCrafts
Online sales
www.lovecrafts.com

Knitting Fever Inc.
www.knittingfever.com

WEBS
www.yarn.com

Jo-Ann Fabric and Craft Stores
Yarns and craft supplies
www.joann.com

Michaels
Craft supplies
www.michaels.com

AUSTRALIA

Black Sheep Wool 'n' Wares
Retail store and online
Tel: +61 (0)2 6779 1196
www.blacksheepwool.com.au

Sun Spun
Retail store (Canterbury, Victoria)
and online
Tel: +61 (0)3 9830 1609
www.sunspun.com.au

If you wish to substitute a different
yarn for the one recommended in
the pattern, try the Yarnsub website
for suggestions: www.yarnsub.com

Acknowledgements

Firstly, I'd love to thank all the makers and crafters who
have supported my creative journey over the years.

Thank you also to the tremendous and talented
team at CICO Books.

Finally, I want to express my gratitude to my
husband, John, and our family for their endless
support and encouragement.